NO ORDINARY ORDINARY BLOKE

HE RESCUED A VILLAGE ... AND SAVED HIMSELF

DONNY PATERSON
WITH NEIL CADIGAN

ABC
Books

The ABC 'Wave' device is a trademark of the Australian Broadcasting Corporation and is used under licence by HarperCollins*Publishers* Australia.

First published in Australia in 2009
by HarperCollins*Publishers* Australia Pty Limited
ABN 36 009 913 517
www.harpercollins.com.au

Text copyright © Donald Paterson and Neil Cadigan 2009

The right of Donald Paterson and Neil Cadigan to be identified as the authors of this work has been asserted by them in accordance with the *Copyright Amendment (Moral Rights) Act 2000*.

This work is copyright. Apart from any use as permitted under the *Copyright Act 1968*, no part may be reproduced, copied, scanned, stored in a retrieval system, recorded, or transmitted, in any form or by any means, without the prior written permission of the publisher.

HarperCollins*Publishers*
25 Ryde Road, Pymble, Sydney, NSW 2073, Australia
31 View Road, Glenfield, Auckland 0627, New Zealand
A 53, Sector 57, Noida, UP, India
77–85 Fulham Palace Road, London W6 8JB, United Kingdom
2 Bloor Street East, 20th floor, Toronto, Ontario M4W 1A8, Canada
10 East 53rd Street, New York NY 10022, USA

National Library of Australia Cataloguing-in-Publication data:

Paterson, Donny.
　No ordinary bloke / Donny Paterson, Neil Cadigan.
　ISBN: 978 0 7333 2565 6
　ABC logo at foot of title.
　Paterson, Donny.
　Disaster relief – Sri Lanka – Peraliya.
　Humanitarian assistance – Sri Lanka – Peraliya.
　Indian Ocean Tsunami, 2004.
　Cadigan, Neil.
　Australian Broadcasting Corporation.
363.349095493

Cover design by Sarah Bull
Internal design by Alicia Freile
Cover photograph of Donny Paterson by Juliet Coombe;
　train and rubble by Shane Schwarz/ Getty Images
Picture section design by Ingrid Kwong
Map by Demap www.demap.com.au
Typeset in 11.5/21pt Minion by Kirby Jones
Printed and bound in Australia by Griffin Press
70gsm Classic used by HarperCollins*Publishers* is a natural, recyclable product made from wood grown in sustainable forests. The manufacturing processes conform to the environmental regulations in the country of origin, Finland.

8 7 6 5 4 3 2 1　　09 10 11 12 13

To the love of my life, Tracey, and our three children. Tracey, you had the courage and conviction and faith in me that the good would resurface; you have kept me alive, and the four of you give me great reason to keep living. I love you so much.

CONTENTS

FOREWORD		1
PREFACE		7
1	SERENDIPITY	13
2	AN UNHAPPY CHILDHOOD	28
3	ESPRIT DE CORPS – BULLSHIT!	51
4	CIVILIAN LIFE	74
5	THE THIRD WAVE	89
6	WE ARE NOT ALONE	118
7	MELTDOWN	140
8	WHEN TWO WORLDS COLLIDE	148
9	A VILLAGE UNDER SIEGE	156
10	THE SECOND COMING	172
11	NEW MAN IN MY OLD WORLD	184
12	MOVIE STARS	196
13	CANNES AND MONTE CARLO	207
14	PERALIYA AND ITS PEOPLE TODAY	222
15	DONNY TODAY	241
16	'IT COULD HAVE BEEN YOUR FUNERAL'	255
A WIFE'S OUTLOOK		263
ACKNOWLEDGEMENTS		273

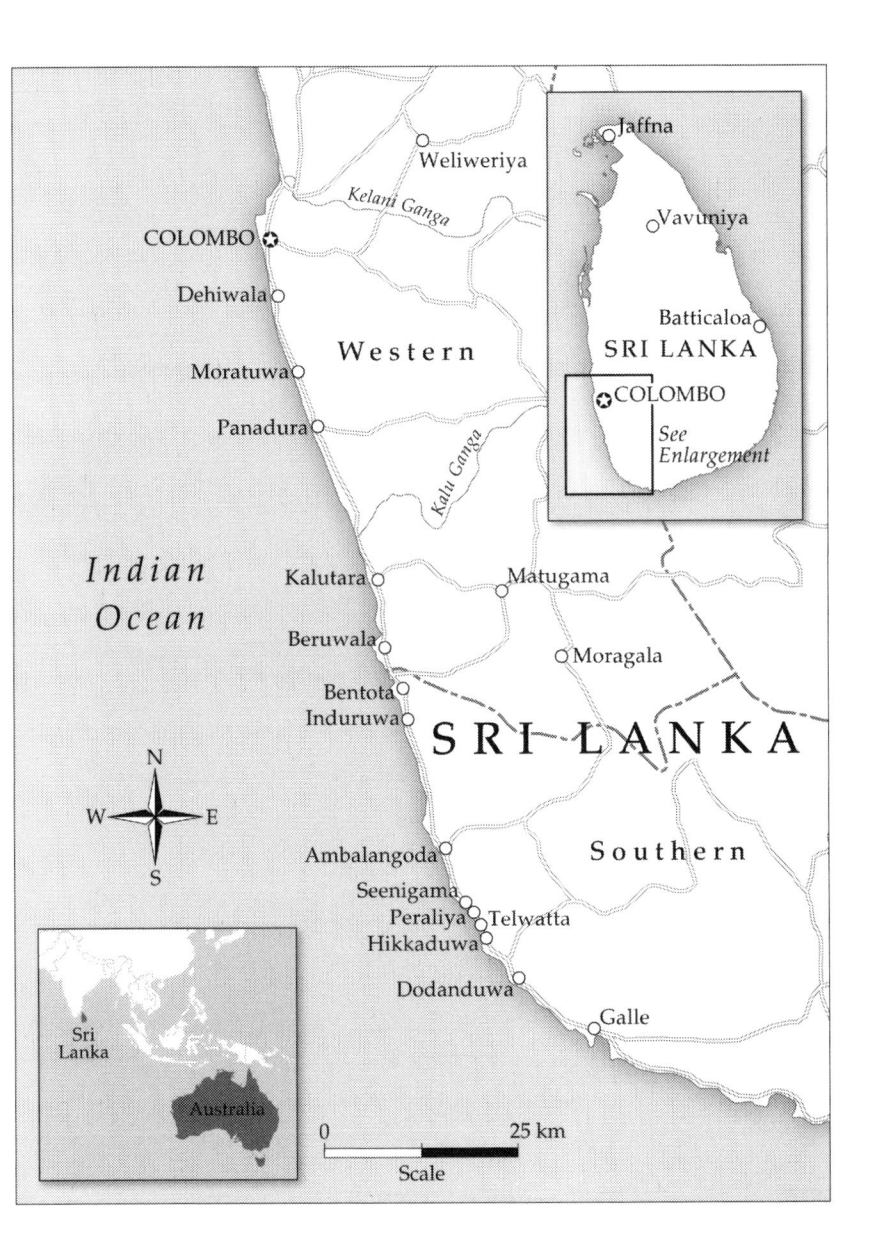

FOREWORD

Cory Paterson, National Rugby League player,
Newcastle Knights

It's pretty cool to be sitting in a bar in San Francisco and one of the world's greatest actors, Sean Penn, says to you: 'Cory, your dad is my hero.' I thought, 'What?' and said something like, 'Yeah, he's a good man, isn't he?' Sean replied, 'Man, your dad's a god.'

It was a surreal moment; I was stunned, really. To be sitting there with Sean Penn and wife, Robyn, in the first place, but to hear him say those sorts of things about my old man? I said I didn't think he was a god, he just liked to help people. But I think Sean couldn't believe how unselfish it was for my old man to have no money and go and leave his family for months to help people far away in the world, people he didn't even know who had been devastated by a tsunami. It really touched Sean; he seemed so intrigued by why someone would do it.

But that's my dad. If you've watched the documentary *The Third Wave*, which shows the post-tsunami experience Dad shared with three people from America, along with others, he's the standout character: the people's champ. He showed his funny side, his sad side, his tough side and his emotional side. And he's real; he swears, he curses, he smokes, he's loud; he wears his Akubra hat and walks around with his big stick to help his wonky knees. He absolutely exposes who he is. I watched the movie with a few Newcastle Knights mates at a premier showing in Newcastle and most of them cried at the end; blokes who are supposed to be tough football heroes wept and looked at me saying, 'That was amazing.' Dad taking off to Sri Lanka and learning to feel good about himself changed his life and our whole family's to some extent. If that hadn't happened, I reckon he'd be dead now, and he admits it in this book.

I like to believe good things happen to good people. To think he stars in a documentary movie, to now have his own book, to have met some famous people … he didn't ask for any of that; it just happened. But very few people know Dad's background: where he came from, how difficult it was for him growing up and how tough he made it for his own family when we were growing up.

He is my hero, too, for overcoming adversity, from being down in the dumps and barely living to being the person he is now. The Donny Paterson of before and the man today are like chalk and cheese. He does so much voluntary work and wants so much to help others. After a Newcastle Knights game I'll go out behind the grandstand and say hello to a heap of people, and most will ask first, 'How's the old man?' and tell me what a character he is; only after that do they ask how I pulled up. I don't mind a bit.

But those people will find out for the first time from reading this book that he wasn't always that man. He loves life so much now because of his past; if he hadn't had those dark days his days wouldn't be so bright today. He had a tough upbringing then had more setbacks when he became addicted to painkilling drugs, and drank too much pretty often too. There were contributing circumstances but that didn't help me, Mum, Karah or Krystal. I learned what was going on from probably the age of ten, and he was the father and husband from hell a lot of the time. Being the oldest, I tried to protect my sisters from knowing what I knew.

In my early teens I'd come home and if I knew he was on the drugs we'd have a row and I would punch holes in the walls. Next day I had to go to school and somehow explain to the teacher why I couldn't write. One time Mum caught him over at the school injecting himself and she came back bawling. I got a knife from the kitchen in a rage; I don't know if I was going to do anything with it but I just thought, 'This is the last time you're going to do this to

Mum and us.' He didn't come home so I was lucky that I didn't have to confront him. I was just sick of Mum being upset and the girls being upset because of that. Mum would confide in me a lot so I was dealing with that and trying to comfort Karah and Krystal too. It was tough; I grew up pretty quickly. I thought if he was not going to be the man of the house, I would be. I became even more determined that with my footy I would make it and support the family.

There were times when Dad was on the drink and he would argue with Mum. The girls would be asleep but I'd wake up and peep in their room. One time Dad threw a beer bottle at Mum; I was only eight or nine. I found my sisters crying and went and cuddled them and told them to block their ears and go to sleep. There was a lot of anger and hurt. I was sick of it; for a while I didn't want a relationship with my father. Most of the time I was pretty good at pretending nothing was wrong. Once I got on the bus to go to school I'd switch it off and be fine, but when I got off the bus to come home I'd wonder what it was going to be like in the house. I'd come in and say hello, then go out and play footy with the kids down the park, come home for dinner then go to bed. I didn't want to deal with it. I could have turned to drugs or alcohol when I was fourteen or fifteen; it was offered to me, but I'd think of what it had done to my old man. It might have been an easy way out but it was the bad way out.

FOREWORD

I wondered at one stage whether it was my fault; whether if I had cleaned my room he wouldn't have blown up or if I wasn't arguing with my sister he might not have snapped. It wasn't; it was a combination of things – his past, his injuries, his depression. And I honestly believe being in the army didn't help him, not the environment of bravado or macho-ism, drinking, smoking, proving yourself to your mates. The army was great to him in some ways but it also built the monster.

We had our good times, too, and we especially loved being involved with rugby league together; that was our bond, our outlet that we enjoyed doing together. But for a lot of years outside of footy, it was pretty rocky between us; I loved him but I didn't like him a lot of the time.

Dad has been a great supporter of my footy, as have been my mum and two sisters. When Dad coached me in the juniors he was hard on me because he didn't want to show any favouritism, which only made me more determined to impress him and that helped me in the end. But if I made a rep side Mum and Dad would do all they could so I could afford the trip and hopefully they could afford to go away to support me too. They would do anything to help any of the three of us out that way; Mum would even pawn her jewellery sometimes. When I wanted to leave Perth to go to Newcastle they were great; they knew it was my dream and they didn't want to deny me that.

These days I think I have a great relationship with my father. As you get older and more mature you understand things better. A lot of that time I didn't think the Donny Paterson I saw was my real dad; it was another character altogether because of the substances he was on. Sometimes when he was 'topped up' he was cheerful, other times he seemed so angry. Now he is that happy medium and I know it's him, not some artificial person caused by medication. I know what to expect all the time. We've had a few scares with his health and I realise I don't want to lose him and lose the good bond we've got now. I have come to grips with the fact that he had a medical problem that he has pretty much beaten and I admire him a lot for that.

He has turned his life around to helping others as his main focus; he has stopped feeling sorry for himself and done some great things, and that's a lesson for a lot of other people. And I reckon he'll keep doing it for a while yet.

He's no god, he's certainly no saint even – just spend half an hour with him and you'll realise that! But he *is* special. That's how I see him. I know thousands of people hero-worship NRL players to some degree, and we have the best supporters in the League at Newcastle, that's for sure. But all I do is play football, a sport I love, and I get paid for it. Dad … well, he doesn't so much save lives as rebuild them. And that's the real hero stuff in my eyes.

PREFACE

Neil Cadigan

Natural disasters and, sadly, terrorist-created disasters seem to have struck much closer to home for us in Australia in the new millennium, figuratively speaking at least. Perhaps that is because the modern electronic media brings graphic images of the devastation into living rooms around the world within minutes of them occurring, ensuring they touch our hearts more deeply and more readily than ever before.

And those events have dominated our media bulletins far too frequently. Amongst them the World Trade Center terrorist attack of 11 September 2001 that claimed over 2000 lives; closer to our shores were the Bali bombings of 12 October 2002, which violently took 202 innocent souls, including 91 Australians. We watched in living colour how Hurricane Katrina, in August 2005, flooded eighty per cent of the American city of New Orleans and claimed 1464 lives. Less than three months before the world's focus would be on the 2008 Olympic Games in Beijing, an earthquake rocked the province of Sichuan, killing almost 70,000.

Most recently, and most tragically for Australia, has been the virtual entrapment of the many who suffered a horrific, fiery death in the Victorian bushfires of February 2009. These were an event which charred the most shocking imprint into Australia's disaster memory with the death toll climbing as this went to press.

The tsunami of Boxing Day 2004 was another that left an indelible impression on our minds, firstly because most of us had never heard the word 'tsunami' before, let alone knew its meaning; and secondly, because the scale of death and tales of devastation were so prolific. An underwater earthquake, its epicentre located off the west coast of Sumatra, Indonesia, read 9.3 on the Richter scale, which makes it the second largest earthquake ever recorded. It triggered a series of tsunamis along thousands of kilometres of Indian Ocean coastline, killing a reported 230,000 people (and probably more) in eleven countries from Indonesia to South Africa, 8000 kilometres from the quake's epicentre. Around one-third of the dead were children. Sri Lanka, Indonesia and the Maldives declared states of emergency while

PREFACE

major holiday resorts in Thailand, thick with tourists (mostly from Europe), were also badly affected. The earthquake generated waves of up to thirty metres high, its vibrations being felt as far away as Alaska.

What made it more dramatic were the shocking images, mostly recorded on the handycams of holiday-makers, that spread around the globe via the internet as well as television, bringing the frightening terror closer to our consciousness than any other calamity except the chilling vision of the collapse of the Twin Towers. The plight of the many affected people prompted a widespread humanitarian response, with the worldwide community pledging more than US$7 billion in aid, although some doubts have been cast on whether all this reached its intended destination, much of the diversion caused by red tape and even alleged corruption by governments, especially that of Sri Lanka.

Many of those who most needed aid and/or funding received little or none. Communities were flooded with help and compassion in the weeks following the two giant waves, only for the world to forget their trauma, loss of livelihoods and ongoing needs after that.

While many of us hopped on the internet or called 1300 numbers to donate some spare cash, others, like Donny Paterson, felt compelled to do more. There are probably scores of Donny

Paterson stories – tales of volunteers who were so moved they took to the air and travelled to affected areas to do what they could to somehow help with the mop-up and give some comfort to the millions of families who lost lives, livelihoods and living quarters. In Sri Lanka alone an estimated 41,000 lives were claimed and 1.5 million lost their homes.

Two stories were prominent among the many hellish recordings of the tsunami's power. One was the overcrowded passenger train in Sri Lanka, fatefully named the *Queen of the Sea*, that was hit from the side by the semitrailer force of the giant wave. The uprising of sea water killed almost all those on board. When the second wave followed, the many from the nearby village of Peraliya who had climbed onto the roofs of the carriages, seeking refuge off the ground, were hit. The other was the tragic tale of Czech modelling beauty Petra Nemcova, who clung to a palm tree for eight hours, despite a broken pelvis and other injuries, to save her life after her fiancé had been swept away to his death. Fate determined that both of those events would intertwine to have a life-changing personal effect on Donny Paterson; they would be part of a series of coincidences that makes his story seem more fiction-like than fact.

However, this book is not just the story of one man's extraordinary journey to a small village located in the maze of affected neighbourhoods, but a real life portrait of the

PREFACE

extraordinary within so many of us that usually lies dormant and is left undisturbed all our lives. An instinct, a hunch, a compelling feeling he can't begin to describe drove Donny to visit Sri Lanka and use the skills he'd learned in an unfulfilled Australian army career to help the lives of people like those he'd seen on his television. The story of a chance meeting with another Australian, albeit one who had called the US her home for many years, and what happened from that moment is compelling enough.

Yet the life of Donny Paterson, before and after those months spent in a deprived, Third World Sri Lankan village, is just as intriguing. It portrays how tragic events had contributed to a downward spiral in his life that he struggled to overcome for years ... then another ignited such a great change of direction that he became the topic of this book and the most endearing character in a documentary film (released in the US this year), which in turn led to his meeting some of the world's wealthiest and best-known public figures. He also happens to be the father of a well-known National Rugby League footballer in Australia, the Newcastle Knights' Cory Paterson.

Perhaps greatest of all, his journey shows that special feats can come from people who appear most ordinary – or, in Donny's case, from someone who saw even much less in himself than that plain description. He is an everyday Australian who had experienced a tough upbringing and more challenges than most, and who felt he had little to offer, only for one single event to change his course and see him inspire thousands of others, as well as himself.

It is a truly remarkable story. Let's begin where fate intercepted his life.

1

SERENDIPITY

It was Boxing Day 2004. To me it started just like any other day. I was dying ... inside at least. That's how I describe it. We'd been in Newcastle just a few months. Our son, Cory, who had been identified as a potential professional footballer, had already been there nearly a year and we'd felt as a family we needed to be together; we'd missed and needed him as much as he did us.

So we were more than happy to move all the way across Australia from Perth, but I hardly knew any bastard; I had no job, bugger-all to occupy myself with and stuff-all to get out of bed for. I'd long before beaten my dependence on prescription drugs and the inclination to hit the booze too much; that was good. But despite taking medication for it, I was in a big hole of depression.

And that's a bad place, let me tell you. You don't want to look at anyone; some days I found it hard even to look at my wife, Tracey, and the kids – Cory, Karah and Krystal. I was still bitter about being medically discharged from the army and the way I was made to feel by the doctors and my fellow soldiers. It's as if I wasn't a worthy person anymore; I had been pigeon-holed as a drug addict. The traumas in my life that had haunted me so badly didn't trouble me as often, but they wouldn't go away. Man, I thought I was going crazy. I look back now and know I wasn't, but that's how I felt at the time.

Boxing Day 2004 certainly didn't end up being any other day. It was *the* day. The day that changed my life. The day that probably saved my life, too, that's how I look at it now. Call it some sort of higher power, if you like, I don't know what it was that hit me but something woke me from my slumber that day and it blows me away how it has affected my life since. And that's what this book is about: no matter how low you think you've sunk, no matter how little self-esteem you have, I believe there is someone worse off, and that there is something in the world for you. I reckon I'm living proof of that.

I was in the bedroom watching TV late in the morning, and dominating the news was this massive earthquake off the Asian coast that caused a tsunami that killed thousands of people. It just woke some inner sense in me. I thought, 'Fuck, how devastating is that, those poor people.' The next day I saw the boss of World Vision Australia, Tim Costello, being interviewed from a place called Galle in Sri Lanka and he was saying there was no aid coming through; he couldn't even get a truck driver to help out because people were too scared to go anywhere near the coast for fear of another giant wave. I thought, 'The least I can do is drive a truck and I can probably help in other ways with my army and first-aid training too. Maybe I should go there.'

I told Tracey that's what I should do, then thought for a minute, 'Yeah, sure, how am I gonna come up with the airfare?', which I found was about two and a half grand. Then the first of two freakish events happened. Tracey was talking to her mother, Betty, who lives in Perth, on the phone that night. Now Betty has always had this sort of talent for premonitions, if you like, and Tracey mentioned something like, 'Did you see the tsunami and how terrible it was?' and told Betty how I was keen to go over and offer some help. Betty responded with something like, 'I was just thinking that sounds like something Donny would do,' and then she offered to pay for the airfare to make it happen.

I'd sent emails to World Vision, the Red Cross and some other aid organisations offering to help but got not one reply – they were obviously overwhelmed and thought what good could this unemployed bloke do? But I had this pressing need to go there. So, as crazy as it seems, I thought, 'Stuff it, I'll just go on my own and get myself to Galle and help all those poor bastards that the world has left behind.' Tracey – now that woman needs a medal for standing by me all these years – was right behind me. And my three kids said, 'Just go, Dad.' I feel very grateful that I was in a position to just drop everything and to have the unselfishness of my family to back me to the hilt. I was also lucky in that I had no job, no hobbies or activities, nothing to have to organise while I was away. There was nothing stopping me. Except me. As it turned out we also had two teenage boys from Perth living with us, trying their hand at the local rugby league competition and the Knights junior representative sides – we were certainly happy to help them out and give them the opportunity Cory had.

I waited until 8 January to leave and the reason was quite simple: I thought by then a lot of the bodies would have been removed. I knew I couldn't cope with that, for reasons I'll explain later (it was too close to the heart). I thought, 'Look, let's give it a week, you know, let the army and everybody else go in there and see what they can do.' I had no specific plans, hardly any money and no bloody idea about the place really, until I researched Sri Lanka on the internet, trying to get a feel for it and its culture.

Tracey drove me the two hours to Sydney airport and nothing much was said. I think there was naturally a lot of trepidation in both our minds about what I was about to embark on and a complete lack of knowledge about what was over there.

Probably, most of all, her concern was about me looking after myself with my antidepression medication and whether the traumatic sights I was naturally about to witness might set me off emotionally again. My fear was simple: 'What if I go all this way over there and they turn me around at the gate?' That was a real possibility, I supposed.

On the plane there were quite a few Sri Lankans going home from Australia to help and find out what had happened to their towns, villages and families. I spoke to as many as I could to get a feel for the place and their people. When I landed at Colombo, the second freakish coincidence happened; call it the hand of God or something, I really don't know, I'm not really religious. I was at the baggage carousel and just a few feet away was a blonde woman, and I said, 'Hi, how are you doing?' and she replied, 'Hi, how are *you* doing?' At first I thought she was an American official from the Red Cross, as she had an American Red Cross key chain around her neck. I thought to myself, 'This might be a good lady to talk to.' We introduced ourselves and I found she was Australian, although she'd been living for years in the US. We got to talking and it turned out both of us had taken it upon ourselves to just head over and see where we could help, so she invited me to join her. That freak meeting with a wonderful woman called Alison Thompson was a godsend for Donny Paterson.

Next her Italian boyfriend Oscar Gubernati appeared and I'm sure he was pretty surprised that Alison had asked this strange Aussie to link up with them. They invited me to tag along with them to their hotel in Colombo and sort of make a bit of a team to head down the coast. They'd already made reservations at the Taj Samudra Hotel, which is a pretty flash hotel, really. They had a friend of a friend landing the next day and had a room booked for him that I could share. I was by myself and had no real idea what my next best move was, so it all sort of made sense. That night about 2 am, a cool dude called Bruce French, who I soon after found out was the touring chef for the bands Red Hot Chilli Peppers, Rush and Pearl Jam, arrived at the hotel. He couldn't get into the room for ages because I was asleep and had the keys inside; great start. His eyes were hanging out of his head, he seemed so tired, but I just got a good vibe from the bloke from the first minute. And my first impression proved absolutely right.

Events of the next few days led the four of us to Peraliya, a village the Sri Lankan government and world aid organisations had pretty much forgotten about until we made them think about the place. It led to us meeting some incredible human beings who came from all parts of the world at their own cost and for their own individual reasons to independently pull off a special aid project following such a terrible natural catastrophe.

It led to us being called gods by the locals, to our story being made into a documentary film that has been shown at the Tribeca and Cannes film festivals, among others, and to me meeting some of the world's most famous people. It enabled me to leave behind the pathetic Donny Paterson who felt no self-worth; it was like a beacon had been switched on in my mind that gave me reason to shake off my depression and devote as much of my life as I could to others, especially those less fortunate. Even talking about it now, you know, I shake my head at how bizarre all this is. Did it really happen to me? If I had stood two metres to the left or right of where I did at Colombo airport's baggage carousel, or I didn't say hi to Alison Thompson, it dead-set wouldn't have happened.

To those who have seen the 'doco' on our experiences, *The Third Wave*, I probably come across as a somewhat larger-than-life Aussie larrikin; a sometimes emotional, highly strung but mostly happy, 'out there' sort of bloke; maybe crazy and a bit demented too, eh? Before Peraliya, that extroverted bloke didn't surface a lot and when he did, it was a charade for the pathetic no-hoper I saw myself as.

On our first day in Colombo we were told where to go to hire a van and a driver, and we met Toyna, who became a very valuable member of our team because he could speak good broken English as well as very good Sinhalese and Tamil. He was one of the better-off Sri Lankans who had a lovely little apartment with his wife and child. I ended up loving him like a brother.

After spending a couple of days acclimatising to the heat and travelling a few kilometres out of Colombo to see places that were absolutely trashed by the tsunami, we headed to Galle with whatever basic medical equipment we'd brought with us or could buy at the supermarket, along with water and snack foods. It is only 97 kilometres from Colombo to Peraliya but over four hours' drive. I'll never forget that first journey. We stopped at a few places along the way and saw some horrifying sights. 'This is almost three weeks after the tsunami hit,' we thought. 'What the hell was it like straight after?' Places were just trashed, buildings flattened, and children everywhere had cuts and bruises that looked like they'd had no medical attention.

I kept a diary for the first couple of weeks of my time in Sri Lanka, and one entry best sums up my initial impressions of the place:

9 January: I was shocked at the damage. Complete devastation. At least two men told me how their children were taken by the sea. Very sad. My fear is that these people, and many more like them, will have watched the aid vehicles drive right by without aiding them. It seems a lot have fallen through the cracks.

We rendered help where we could. The first village we pulled into I gave out some toothbrushes and cigarettes. Well I was mobbed. Simple bloody objects which are accepted as part of our daily routine were, for these people, an absolute luxury. They flocked around me like I was giving out gold to the poor or luxury food to the starving. And I learned pretty quickly after that that the things we just took for granted in life – like fresh water, somewhere to go to the toilet, somewhere to sleep, something to eat – these people had literally had flushed away in the tsunami. At another town we stopped at, Beruwala, all the children were walking around in a sort of daze; none of them was laughing or playing, or had any joy in them at all, like you would normally expect from innocent kids who are so often unfazed by events around them. But on this day they all seemed so glum. So I got out a heap of 'tazos' I had brought from Australia – you know, those little collector cards kids usually go berserk for – and finally I got a reaction and some smiles from them. For a few moments anyway.

A little further down the coast we stopped at Bentota and I will never forget the sight there that really brought home to me how poor the country was: medical gloves from the hospital hanging on a clothes line, drying so they could be used again. They couldn't even afford new latex gloves! The equipment was very old, almost antique some of it, and they had coconut husks packed into sheets to make a mattress. I treated about ten men that day with injuries ranging from sprained ankles to a very nasty compound fracture of the collarbone. My diary tells another story:

> *11 January: Just visited another village at Induruwa. Treated a man with a very badly lacerated foot, could have done with about 10 stitches. Also treated a lady with a bad burn on her calf. Treated others for aches and pains. These people were so appreciative they climbed a coconut tree and gave me one, a very special moment. I've just seen my first corpse, a 12 to 14 year old child badly decomposed and headless. On a brighter note I rescued a baby turtle from a well and released it in the ocean.*

As we ran into other Westerners we were getting reports that the further south we went, the worse it was. Still we intended to go all the way to Galle, the main town along the south-western coastline. We were at a town called Ambalangoda when we ran into two pilots, a Kiwi, Steve, and a British guy, Luke, who were also well trained in first aid. They were going down there to help for a few days, so we followed them. They told us about this place called Peraliya. They said there was no help there, the whole town had been destroyed, and it was where the train *Queen of the Sea* had been hit and just about every passenger on board its eight carriages (1643, in fact) had been wiped out. We never got to Galle. Instead we made Peraliya, what little there was left of it anyway, our home away from home. Its people, and the many thoughtful souls that came to help them over the ensuing weeks, became our adopted families. It was a hellhole in paradise.

We hit the village late in the afternoon on a stifling hot day. What a sight. The coral reef in front of the village had been ravaged over the years, like a few places along the Sri Lankan coast, as a means of surviving. Some was cleared out for paths for the fishing boats, a lot of it sold as ornaments; I also saw many pieces which had been used as building material. There was a theory that the removal of so much of the natural reef made Peraliya more exposed to the tsunami because it had no natural barrier to slow the waves. Two miles further along the coast the tourist village of Hikkaduwa was not nearly as badly affected. Peraliya? Man, it was wiped out like the front pin in a ten-pin bowling alley. Strike!

Four things probably best sum up my initial impressions of Peraliya. Firstly, the smell. The smell of death. It became all too familiar those first few days. Most of the 2000 corpses had been pulled off the ground or out of the rubble and put into a big mass grave or, for those lucky enough to have been identified by relatives, buried next to their homes. The stench of dead bodies in the rubble and the lack of sanitation was bloody awful. Then there was the train, the *Queen of the Sea*. It was overcrowded with people, most on their way home from Colombo or on the way to a coastal holiday. When the first wave hit, the passengers either drowned or were trapped as the train tilted over. Apparently many of the remaining villagers jumped onto its roof thinking they were safe. Then the second wave hit and wiped them out; the bodies of some were found miles inland. It had been put back on the tracks by the time we arrived and at first glance it looked pretty much like a normal train, save for some battered body work. It was serene almost. It had become a sort of surreal shrine for the families of those who had perished, or a tourist hot-spot, and many people would pass by, take photos and move on, which I found pretty galling; there were people desperate for a few rupees or a bottle of water or any sort of help, and the tourists just took a souvenir shot and left. In the end we used the fascination with the train, which stood right next to the main road to Galle, to our advantage and got the kids to sort of funnel passers-by to it and ask for water or donations which went into our 'mission'.

Next, I noticed there were two buildings left standing – the school library and one school building. In the rest of the village there might have been ten houses still upright to some degree, including the temple which we knew we had to clean out as soon as we could so the people could mourn there. Everything else was just flattened as far as the eye could see. The library – about six metres by seven metres in size – became what I called the 'heart' of Peraliya – the place where we had our daily meetings with the elders, the makeshift hospital, the kitchen and temporary dormitory for the homeless. I thought, 'How could the library and the temple still be erect, like two dominoes standing when all the others folded to the floor?' It didn't make sense, but then again not much did.

Lastly, and still most vivid to this day from my first day in Peraliya, were the faces of the people. They were expressionless, empty, hopeless-looking faces of people meandering aimlessly around what used to be their village. Someone had cleared a lot of the debris and shattered pieces of the buildings to form a sort of quadrangle around the library, and hundreds of people were just walking around it, or sitting in the sun, like zombies. This was two and a half weeks after the tsunami had hit and they'd had no help from outside and had little idea how to help themselves. So many of them had had almost all their family wiped out; kids were walking aimlessly without any brothers or sisters or parents left. They had no water, no toilets and were lucky to get a couple of handfuls of rice and dhal to get through the day. People were crying over lost ones, crying over the little they had left. 'Fuck man,' I said to myself, 'what the hell did you have to be depressed about!' Looking back now, that was a pivotal point in my life and the first instance of recognition that I really had nothing to be depressed about. These people had nothing. From that day I not only pledged to help them but also to take stock of my own life and re-examine myself and why I was so down on myself.

There were four of us when we left Colombo, six by the time we decided to set down our roots. The plan was to stay for just a week or so – at Peraliya. Steve and Luke had to get back to work a few days later, so then there were four. But word got out via a website Alison set up, and after a couple of weeks some wonderful people came to help from all over the world. The days grew into weeks, then months. Those zombies became real people – not always nice people because in desperate times people do desperate things – and those dazed looks turned into smiles. Ah, the smiles of those kids despite them having absolutely nothing; they will be with me for as long as I live.

I'll take you through the story of this small part of Sri Lanka, and my life too, because the correlation between the two is more uncanny than I could possibly have ever realised. Peraliya had lost hope, and so had I. Its people got through their days in a daze, as I often did. Its people are grateful for the role I played in turning around their lives, but they have little idea of just how grateful I am for their help in turning my life around.

Before I introduce you to Peraliya, post-tsunami in early 2005, I'd better introduce you to Donny Paterson, pre-tsunami.

It also isn't a pretty story. It contains some heavy shit that those who were with me in Sri Lanka had no idea about; in fact a lot of my family and closest friends won't even know until they read this.

2

AN UNHAPPY CHILDHOOD

When I arrived in Colombo I had one large backpack and a suitcase of supplies that I thought might help the needy. But what could not be seen by Alison, Oscar or anyone else at the airport luggage carousel was the baggage I was carrying inside. I didn't carry as big a load of that psychological excess baggage on my return plane trip; I was miraculously able to offload a good part of it in a place called Peraliya … but not all. Some will be with me all my life.

I didn't have a particularly happy childhood before I left school at fifteen and joined the army at seventeen, hoping to achieve a sense of being wanted, valued and respected for the first time in my life.

AN UNHAPPY CHILDHOOD

I can't say I don't have any fond memories of growing up, I have – but not nearly as many as most people, I reckon. When you live in thirty different towns before you turn seventeen, have a mother who was addicted to prescription drugs and a father who never showed any real affection, it's easy to feel unwanted and unaccepted. You can't ever get those impressionable years back, you can only use the lessons you learned in your own parenting, which I have tried to do – when I was able. Falling into habits similar to my mother's with prescription drugs made it very hard at times; the irony is tragic, really. I thought she was just a weak person and I went from loving her so much as a young child to hating and resenting her. Now, I realise she just needed someone to help, someone to understand. But it's hard to live with someone who suffers a sickness like that. Again old Donny Paterson is living proof, from when I was a child and later when I was an adult.

Mum died when she was forty-two, the same age I am now. It was too young, too sad. I'm not sure when Mum turned to the pills. It was only in a recent conversation with my father that I learned she had a hysterectomy that went wrong and further surgery associated with the complications, causing her a lot of pain and grief and for a while she needed relief; it must have affected her badly. The old man is still alive but, as much as I've tried, we don't have any real sort of relationship and I think it's sad he's missing out on seeing his grandchildren grow up.

Anyway, a bit of my story, of my struggles. I was born on 20 July 1966 in Bowral, New South Wales – just over a year after my sister Christeen. My father, Thomas, was a tough Scotsman from Glasgow and my mum, Thelma Perry, was from New South Wales. We lived then at a place called Braemar in the state's Southern Highlands, but before I'd left school I'd also lived in many other places across two states as my dad went from job to job as a market gardener or a worker on properties: Braemar, Mittagong, Berrima and Bowral in the Southern Highlands; Rookwood (where Dad worked as a gardener at the war graves), Riverstone, Ermington, Luddenham and Penrith in Sydney; Dandenong and Keilor in Victoria; Medlow Bath, Lawson and Bullaburra in the NSW Blue Mountains and Canowindra in the central-west. After I left school and before I went into the army there were also Meadowbank and Manly in Sydney and Orange out west. They're the places I remember anyway; the old man once counted thirty places by the time I became a soldier. That's a lot of schools, a lot of making friends and saying goodbye to them, a lot of wondering, 'What the hell is the next place going to be like?'

I could find trouble when I was a kid, when it came to hurting myself anyway. I remember an incident in which I was rushed to hospital; apparently I had gotten into some pills from on top of the fridge – Mum's, I assume. Anyway, all I remember is lying on the hospital bed getting my stomach pumped. Another time Christeen and I were wandering around the service station next to us run by a bloke we called Uncle Bill, who used to make concrete garden gnomes and the like, and a concrete fish pond fell on me and broke my leg. I was probably four years old. Then there was the time I spent seven days in hospital due to an allergic reaction to penicillin; my whole body swelled up in big welts. The diagnosis today would be anaphylactic shock.

I recall getting belted quite a bit as a young fella and nothing was good enough for my parents. I felt like I had to prove myself to them all the time. I remember Mum beating me with the jug cord more than once; that thing would leave big bloody welts on my skin. Others times she'd go off like a firecracker and begin beating me badly with a wooden spoon, like an animal in sheer rage. When we were living in a flat at Dandenong, just outside of Melbourne in Victoria, I ran away from home because I had had an accident in the toilet and I got flogged and made to feel dirty. I rode the train and walked around Melbourne for about ten hours before the police found me. I got scared as soon as it got dark and just wanted to go home anyway.

From there we went to Riverstone in Sydney's western suburbs, which doesn't hold many good memories. I remember that Mum would always look groggy and out of it, and she and Dad would fight a lot, mainly because Dad was so frustrated by Mum's addiction and really had no idea how to get her to quit. From there we moved to a lice- and flea-infested rented house in Ermington on Victoria Road, a main arterial route out of Sydney. I remember not being able to sleep for the fleas. Then we moved to a small farm at Luddenham, then to another flat in Penrith where finally I liked the school and started playing rugby league, which I loved. Footy become a real saviour for me later in life, and the greatest thing to bond my son, Cory, and me over the years. I think I might have been not half bad if I had had the support of my parents; they very rarely ever came to watch me play sport and I often had to find my own way to training and to games, although I remember them coming to a game of hockey I was playing in once. I guess I was just mediocre in my sporting abilities but I do believe, though, that it is practically impossible for kids to make it in any sport without 100 per cent support and help from their parents.

We moved to Medlow Bath in the Blue Mountains, which is famous for the Hydro Majestic Hotel, where both my parents worked for a while. I really enjoyed attending Blackheath Primary School and my one moment of fame came when I was elected as the best reader in my class and was given the honour of reading a scroll to the Queen of the Rhododendron Festival in front of an audience; the festival is a big annual event in Blackheath. I had to dress up in page boy regalia. I remember thinking I looked a bit of a twit and that stockings didn't do anything for me. Anyway I got to ride in the horse and cart with the queen to the park where I met the Prime Minister, Mr Gough Whitlam. I remember him telling me I had done a 'splendid job'. I think I was probably nine or ten at the time.

From Medlow Bath we moved to Keilor in Victoria, where Dad worked at a big market garden; a good memory was going out into the fields picking capsicums and eating them just like apples. A bad memory was getting caught pinching a packet of chewing gum and the shop owner racing after me and scooping me up before I could get far. Mum came and picked me up. I wasn't allowed to have dinner that night or have blankets on my bed. 'Thieves don't have those luxuries,' said Dad. I don't know how I didn't get hypothermia.

When we moved to Lawson in the Blue Mountains I had my first real mentor in my teacher, Mr Lehooray. I spent more time at this school than any other – one and a half years. It was at Lawson that we were hit by the terrible experience of raging bushfires, something too familiar to the Blue Mountains area. Dad and I went out in his flat-bed truck to get something at the shops and by the time we got back the fires were threatening our street. We were able to get back to our house and these huge flames seemed just a few metres away, which was frightening for a nine-year-old. I panicked and I remember Dad gave me a good smack in the face to calm me down. We got all we could into Dad's flat-bed and

Mum's car and evacuated to a refuge in the main street of Lawson while Dad and a milkman returned to save our house – the milk depot was across the road. A lot of homes were burnt down and one girl from our area died in the fires. It was a pretty traumatic year. Not long after, my mum lost her younger sister, Aunty Dianne, who was killed when a drunk driver hit her while she was changing a tyre on the Pacific Highway near Old Sydney Town on the Central Coast, north of Sydney. The guy was so pissed he ran over her twice! Mum really hit the pills after that.

I always wanted to be in the army or other services and was always playing with toy soldiers when I was a kid. While attending Katoomba High School I joined the cadets and had my first taste of the military. The day I received my uniform I got off the school bus and went into the bush and got changed. I felt really proud so I strolled into the house and Mum and Dad were really happy; for the first time in my life I felt that I had made a great achievement. We used to go on weekend camps – bivouacs – with the cadets and paraded once a week after school and did things like drill and field craft. I really enjoyed the cadets, it gave me a sense of belonging and purpose. When we went on our Annual Field Exercise we would get to shoot rifles and be just like junior soldiers. The cadets were a great way for me to escape from the normal, everyday life I was living. It also put me in good stead to join the army, which I had decided was going to be my career.

AN UNHAPPY CHILDHOOD

Cadet camps were held annually at Singleton Army Camp for two weeks and on one particular camp I was sexually abused by a commanding officer of the unit. We were sitting beneath a tree, talking about my promotion to lance corporal, when he started to rub my chest. At the time I thought it was just his way of showing his care. He then proceeded to touch my private parts, telling me I shouldn't say anything to anybody because it might jeopardise my chance for promotion. I felt it was wrong so I stopped him and just then, luckily for me, the rest of the guys returned. I never thought any more about it. I didn't know anything about sex and hadn't even reached puberty. Strangely, I think it made me feel wanted. Years later I found out that this guy had been busted for pedophilia and stood down from his job, and that's when a rage came over me as I realised who he was and what he had tried to do to me, and I wondered how many other teenage boys he had violated.

I did get promoted that weekend, and that caused more drama. A good mate, David, was pissed off because I beat him for the promotion (if I'd resisted the commanding officer's touching I wonder if Dave would have been promoted over me, or whether he tried anything on Dave, too, and he resisted). A group of us went on our Annual Field Exercise and one night I was ambushed by a person wearing a balaclava who jumped out from behind a tree and proceeded to beat me. A search of the area found nobody who shouldn't have been there. We later learned that it was Dave's bigger brother who beat me up because I got promoted over Dave.

My parents split up for the first time when we were living on a farm at Canowindra when I was fourteen. I went to live with Dad and Christeen went with Mum. The next few years we constantly relocated, Mum and Christeen coming back and leaving again before I eventually left school, and later home. I couldn't get away from the old man quick enough; he never once showed me any kind of love, really. He was a pretty cold, set-in-his-ways kind of bloke, and you couldn't change his mind about anything. If he thought you had done something wrong he would punish you severely. To this day I wonder why my dad is the way he is; I can't work it out.

I left school as soon as I turned fifteen and floated from job to job. I was knocked back as an apprentice in one of the trades on offer because, I was told, I was too immature, then I tried to get an apprenticeship in the navy at fifteen but was knocked back (entry for all the other services was age seventeen). We were living in Meadowbank in Sydney when I left home for the first time and went and lived with my footy coach's daughter, who, I found out, was a prostitute; my old man ordered me out of the place pretty quickly after that. I joined the Army Reserve and I had lots of friends, a few bob and I didn't have to answer to anybody except me. I felt independent, a big man if you like, then at seventeen I joined the Australian Regular Army determined to make something of my life. I was in Orange by then – Mum and Christeen were living in a flat and Dad was living in the back of a Pantec truck at a friend's place.

I wanted to be a soldier more than anything in the world. I wanted my parents and sister to be proud of me and for people to take notice of me. I liked the idea of camaraderie too, and this wonderful culture of 'esprit de corps', which proved to be bullshit, although I've still got mates all over Australia from those army days, which is one positive legacy. Two of them I keep in regular contact with are Michael Cuerden and Mark Burnett, who have been great mates and supporters in tough times. Michael was one of my first mentors during my army days; a humorous guy who used to run amok at times, with me a willing ally.

On 27 June 1984 I was sworn in to the armed forces, the proudest moment of my life, and was put onto the bus with other unsuspecting recruits for our eighty days of training at Kapooka. Mum and Dad were at the defence recruiting building near Central Station in Sydney to wave me off and I could tell they were very proud of me; for once I thought I had done something right. I remember getting on the bus and seeing Mum and Dad waving. Mum was crying a lot and Dad had his arm around her. It was a rare happy family moment that I can remember.

I'll never forget arriving on that bus full of would-be soldiers at Kapooka, the army training facility near Wagga Wagga in New South Wales. The first thing the troop sergeant said to us, after calling us a bunch of maggots, was something like: 'Okay, if you fuckers want to cut your wrists, cut downwards and not crossways; you'll bleed out quicker that way.' I thought, 'What have I got myself into here? He's telling us how to commit suicide!' You soon got used to that sort of talk, though. They were tough bastards, the sergeants, and that's what their job was – to try to break us, push us to our limits and weed out those who they thought wouldn't make good soldiers.

It was at Kapooka that I celebrated my eighteenth birthday and got pissed. At the end of our duties week we were allowed to go and have a barbecue at the lake and it happened to coincide with my birthday. We were allowed two cans of beer each but the guys who didn't drink gave me their rations and I proceeded to get horribly drunk. I really enjoyed myself because I was the centre of attention and it felt good having people around who cared, or who appeared to care.

It was great to wear jungle greens, get fitter than I'd ever been and feel as though I'd passed a real test in life by coping with the highly disciplined, regimented lifestyle. And that's what it was, over the top really. If your bedclothes had one crease in them or you had not made your bed properly, the bedclothes would be dismantled and thrown out the window from our third floor quarters and we'd have to go and retrieve them, bring them up three flights of stairs and start again. Reveille was at 5.30 am, breakfast at 6, and then we'd do physical training for an hour or more. We had a sergeant, Sergeant Payne, who used to bellow, 'My *name* can also be my *nature*.' Shit, he used to flog us. Part of the training included weapons training; standing on the drills square doing drills for two or three hours straight; learning camouflage and concealing techniques, navigation and how to patrol as a group. They weren't teaching us to be circus performers! In those days you had to lift your feet up to the height of your GP (general purpose) boot and slam them down again when you did a change of direction. It's no wonder blokes have got screwed knees and backs – we had to run in Dunlop Volleys, which were the issued shoes, and they didn't help your joints either. They were great for gardening or tennis but not for marching or running.

After I completed the training, Mum and Dad were at the passing out parade at Kapooka and that day I had a drink with the old man for the first time. After deciding I wanted to become a Royal Australian Engineer I marched into the School of Military Engineering in Moorebank in Sydney's south-west, where I spent ten months. I liked the idea of being a combat field engineer, thinking I'd get to play with a lot of explosives and make things go bang. There's nothing more powerful than watching a demolition charge go off knowing you had just made that happen. As well as that there were many other jobs on offer within the corps. I got landed with a storeman's role but at least I was qualified as an engineer and could swap over to being that later on. I became Sapper Paterson (sapper was the bottom rank in the engineers, equivalent to a private). The word 'sap' means to undermine — it was used in World War I to describe those who had to dig trenches on the front line, so the word was extended to 'sapper'.

I still had a tendency to land in some bother. I was working at the bridging yard at the School of Military Engineering where there were also civilians working, and one day this bloke — we didn't get on and something had been building for a while to be honest — called me a bastard, as in I didn't know my parents rather than a term to suggest I was a prick. Being the young upstart that I was, I saw red and punched him fair on the nose. He reported me to the regimental sergeant major who told me to prepare to go to jail after seeing the commanding officer. Shit, a stint in jail for punching some spineless civilian I worked with? I finished work, went to the boozer and drank a 1.25-litre bottle of scotch on my own. My mate Banksy also sank a bottle of scotch and after staggering into the shower block at the barracks we got into a fight and I smashed his nose, too, and he went off to hospital for the night! I was still pissed the next day when I had to face the 'old man', Lieutenant Colonel Rose, who was the commanding officer. I can remember it vividly today. You had to take your hat and belt off, stand to attention at his desk, and listen to the decided punishment – you didn't get a chance to defend yourself or add your point of view.

'Good morning.'

'Good morning, sir.' I didn't salute as I didn't have my hat on.

'Sapper Paterson, you have been charged with assault. I award you 168 hours detention at the military corrective establishment.'

That was it, in and out; no right of reply, couldn't plead my case or mention any mitigating circumstances. And the hours were counted exactly from the time you walked in, so it was 3 am when my 168 hours were completed and I was woken and marched out of the joint. Getting through that time in the corrective establishment was the toughest thing I had done, the longest week of my life. You couldn't talk to anyone outside a fifteen-minute period at night when you could read a magazine and talk in a group. You were allowed only three cigarettes a day and had to stand at attention to smoke; you had to run everywhere instead of walking; they'd get you on the drill square and just flog you with the drills for hour upon endless hour. Everything was made of brass, of course – every shower, tap, pipe and knick-knack. And you know what you do with brass in the army, you polish it; you'd polish brass all bloody day.

We weren't allowed to sit on our beds at night-time when they locked us in; we had to sit on the cold masonite floor (it was winter) and we couldn't get into bed until lights out. When you got up in the morning all your sheets and blankets had to be folded immaculately in a perfect square; if one bit was out of whack the noncommissioned officers (sergeants and corporals) would destroy it and you had to do it all again. Your shirts had to be hung the same way, with a certain amount of room between each one; if any was a millimetre out they'd trash your shirts and you had to line them up again. Your shoes had to be highly polished whether you had used them or not, and had to be lined up a certain distance from the wall, exactly. I don't think they would get away with those sorts of disciplinary measures today, or the physical and mental anguish you were put through as a soldier in the 1980s. I certainly learned a lesson from that very difficult week: keep your hands to yourself no matter what sort of moron has pissed you off!

I fixed up that civilian prick who caused me to explode and spend that time in the corrective establishment. I knew he bought lottery tickets each week so I rang him and put on a voice and told him I was from the lotteries office and he'd won $25,000; I said I would meet him that evening to hand over his cheque. You could hear him hooting and hollering in jubilation and the poor bastard had a massive smile on his face when he went down for the 'appointment' – and waited around for an hour before the penny dropped that he had been 'had'. I don't know if he ever suspected me.

A field engineer in the army has a wide range of tasks including but not limited to: demolition, mine warfare, booby traps, box culverts, preparing landing zones for helicopters, fixing up destroyed air fields and constructing buildings. Within the engineer corps there are plant operators, carpenters, electricians and plumbers. We were basically the army's construction and demolition arm.

I finished my IET (Initial Employment Training) course, in other words I'd done my training to be a field engineer after going through basic training to be a soldier at Kapooka, and got posted to the 22 Construction Squadron at Karrakatta in Perth, which would be my home base for the next five years. It was 1985 and I was nineteen. I had to bunk with a fellow called Emu and I quickly discovered how he got the nickname: one, he had a surname that was too hard to pronounce or spell and, two, he could drink the local brew – Emu Lager – like no other man on earth. He passed away a few years ago now, but I'll always have fond memories of him; RIP Emu.

By day my roles alternated between that of a storeman, which meant looking after technical gear and clothing, and doing field exercises. At night, well Thursdays through to Saturday or Sunday each week or fortnight, it was out for a few drinks and to find girls. And I did just that one night – 22 August 1985, thanks, Tracey – at Shafto's on Shafto Lane. I was with my mate Swanny (Bill Swanson) and 'Nifty' Palmer and saw Tracey at the bar and, I think, gestured for her to come over and chat. She was with a group of friends that night and she reckons my eyes were the things that attracted her. Within a week I was in love with her. I reckon I was looking for someone in my life then: I'd had enough time around the lads only.

Tracey was a £10 Pom immigrant, coming out to Australia with her parents from Liverpool when she was six. She was actually waiting to join the army at the time; how ironic is that? She'd done all her entrance tests and was due to fly out that December to Kapooka in the next intake, after delaying her trip because her grandfather had been ill – sadly he died shortly after we met. We became pretty serious on each other quite quickly, and I probably talked her out of leaving Perth and doing the training.

When the pub shut we went two doors up to a bar and I sauntered over to the jukebox, put a coin in and told Tracey this song was for her: 'Talking to an Angel' by the Eurythmics. Pretty cool, eh? Tracey must have thought so, too, because as she was returning from the toilet Swanny cornered her and put it on her: 'Okay, which one do you like, eh?' and she replied, 'Sorry, not you, the other bloke.' At the end of the night Tracey was the only one with a car so we bludged a lift back to the barracks with her, but only after we stopped at Kings Park overlooking the city. I was giving her my best chat-up lines while Swanny and Nifty played combat, 'shooting' each other and rolling down the hill. I asked Tracey out to the pictures the next night but instead we went to Fremantle Markets. Now, talk about a girl finding a way for a bloke to stay overnight. Tracey's dog peed over my legs so I had to change my trousers and have them washed. That meant changing into Tracey's pink dressing gown – now how could she not be turned on by that? – and I stayed the night until my clothes were dry. True story.

We moved in together a few months later but, as per most of my life, there was a drama there too. Tracey's flatmate's boyfriend was a bit of a jerk and one day he was trying to aggravate me and get me to fight him. Next thing he went outside and kept calling me to front up to him. I was in uniform and didn't want to get into trouble again by bashing a civilian – been there, done that – until he had a go at the Queen. I was very proud of the Queen, the army and the uniform and all those things then, so I saw red and went out and gave him a flogging. He got up off the footpath, walked straight inside and called the police. They came out and rather than arrest me they gave me a summons to appear in court, which I did. I got fined $80 but had no conviction. I still don't have a criminal record in civilian life, although my military resumé is a bit checkered! Anyway, Tracey decided to move out and needed somewhere to live; I was staying over a bit anyway and didn't drive a car, so we thought, 'Why not move in together?'

Less than three months after we'd been going out, Tracey became pregnant, but we decided, after a lot of uncertainty and heartache, for her to have an abortion. It was only about twelve months later when she fell pregnant again. By this time our relationship was rock solid and we'd planned to get married in November of 1987 anyway, so we brought it forward to 3 January – seventeen months after we'd met. Tracey looked beautiful and I felt pretty handsome in my military uniform too. The only thing that marred the day was that Mum and Dad weren't there – well, other than the fact that I had to wear a back-brace because of an injury I suffered playing cricket during inter-service sport, which saw me in hospital for forty-one days, most of it in traction.

That back injury, and the resulting forty-one days in hospital, was a defining period in my life, as it turned out. I was on morphine for most of those six weeks to nullify the terrible pain: my first introduction to narcotics. It was some time before I became addicted to narcotics but certainly the feeling of euphoria during that period made me vulnerable to my later trauma with drugs. That back injury was the start of it all.

It wasn't long into our marriage that I had my second major blow-up with army authority. We were at the Bindoon training area about eighty kilometres from Perth. We were building a campsite, a virtual small town, out of virgin bush as part of an urban assault range to be used by the SAS (Special Air Service). It was a Friday night and some of us were having a few drinks with another unit, unfortunately it was rum after I'd had a few beers in our tent. I had the use of a Land Rover to run meals from one camp to another and after doing the food run and having a few drinks at the canteen I decided to drive into town to ring Tracey because she was eight months pregnant. I never made it to town.

I was about fifteen kilometres from the base and these kangaroos came out from nowhere. I swerved, lost control and rolled the Land Rover quite a few times. I didn't have a seatbelt on and was thrown from the vehicle, which might have saved my life. I was out in the middle of nowhere and it was freezing. I walked probably three kilometres and was in too much pain and too exhausted to go any further. I remember trying to start a fire using paper from my wallet, including money, to keep warm. I dead-set thought I was going to freeze to death. A truck driver eventually picked me up early the next morning and took me to the local hospital at Toodjay. I was transferred to one of the main hospitals in Perth where I spent a few days recovering. I broke three ribs and punctured my lung, but I was a very lucky young man; I was told that had I had a seatbelt on I wouldn't have come out of it alive.

I then had to face the music and my punishment was fourteen days confined to barracks – because I took the Land Rover out of the area without permission and because I had been drinking – plus I was ordered to pay $680 restitution for damage to the Land Rover (presumably it was covered by insurance). I was pretty lucky, I thought – until quite a few months later when the army decided to double dip and ordered me to repay the total amount of money it cost to repair the vehicle, which was $5283.02. I ended up organising to pay $20 out of my fortnightly pay and was still paying off the debt, which had a very high rate of interest in those days, when I was discharged from the army a decade later. And I tell you, I have never been guilty of drink driving since.

Cory was born in July 1987, a great day in our lives. Things were going well for Tracey and me then, although she often reckoned I was drinking too much. It wasn't like every night but bingeing with the other guys in uniform; it was as much peer group pressure as anything else. I was twenty-one and married with a child but part of me still wanted to be one of the boys and do what they were doing all the time. If I went for a drink, it would end up a big drink. And that was part of army culture too. We'd had a 'sport' session every Thursday, which didn't always involve physical exertion; one of my first 'sporties' was a tit-show at a pub. Once a month we'd knock off at three instead of four in

AN UNHAPPY CHILDHOOD

the afternoon and go to the unit's boozer as a group. Some would go for an hour or two but most would make it into a 'big one' – and I wouldn't want to miss out on that. So drinking with the boys was certainly encouraged, although I believe it has changed dramatically in today's army.

And in typical Donny fashion, the grog got me into all sorts of strife come Christmas that year. Here is another episode I'm not proud of but it typifies the rough edges in my character – and should be in the manual of how not to impress a father-in-law! Tracey's dad, Jim, and his new wife, Lillian, flew over from England to meet me and see baby Cory for the first time, and spend a nice warm Christmas with us in Perth. Her parents had split up years before and Jim had gone back to England while her mother stayed in Geraldton. Anyway, everything was going well, we had a great Christmas Day and a few beers, of course. On Boxing Day we had a few more and I ended up sitting on the front fence of our place discussing the attributes of life Down Under with the father-in-law. I was so pissed I couldn't remember the conversation but evidently I told him I only married Tracey because she was pregnant. I don't know what was going through my head – maybe I resented that I was missing out on the wild life mates my age were enjoying. I didn't mean it, that's for sure. Tracey's dad blew up and told me to piss off. He immediately reported the conversation to Tracey, who said I could clear out.

So I went to live in the barracks for two or three months before she would have me back.

When we got back together it was something way beyond our marital relationship that set me off again – two shocking events that would change my life, for the worse, and take until that time in Peraliya many years later before I could genuinely come to grips with them – and they happened nowhere near the battlefield I'd been trained to survive in.

3

ESPRIT DE CORPS – BULLSHIT!

Nothing could have prepared me for it. It was like a scene from a horror movie and that scene has haunted my mind ever since, a recurring nightmare that I just can't escape. His name was Simon. You know, I've never learned his last name. He'd have a son or daughter who'd be twenty-one by now who has never known his or her father. Then there was the other bloke, who was almost decapitated. Unlike Simon, he was dead before I got to him.

I know what you're thinking – it must be tough seeing a soldier die in battle. But I never saw any action in uniform. This was right outside our home in suburban Perth, and Tracey reckons that maybe because I wasn't in uniform, wasn't in army 'cope with it, soldier, that's what you're trained for' mode, that it affected me more than it might have. I have never thought of it that way and disagree with Tracey on that, to be honest. Witnessing those two events sent me on a downward spiral that took a tsunami to finally shake me out of.

I was sitting at home in Karinyup watching TV when I heard this God almighty bang outside. I raced outside and the scene before me was horrifying. There were power lines down everywhere, three cars smashed up and this guy in his twenties walking around in a daze. We lived on the main street that led to the beach right next to a busy crossroad. Two blokes in one of the cars had apparently been out looking for a missing dog and their vehicle went down a hill, straight through a stop sign, hit a work van travelling on the other street and, it appears, ricocheted off it into a power pole. The van was pushed into a parked car and a wheel from one of the vehicles had gone through the wall of a house.

Tracey followed me out to see if she could help and I screamed at her to go back inside with Cory; I didn't want her to see such a depressing sight and was worried about her being around the live electricity wires. I inspected the scene carefully and saw a guy who I presumed was the driver of the vehicle wandering around in a daze, calling out, 'Simon, Simon, where are you?' In my loudest 'sergeant major' voice I yelled at him to stop still, sit on the ground and not move, because I was worried about him wandering into some live wires. Fortunately he heeded my words.

I moved closer to the crash scene and came across Simon, who had been thrown clear of the car into a tree trunk. He was unconscious and I crouched over him and applied the COW method, asking, 'Can you hear me? Open your eyes. What's your name?' He just lay there motionless. I managed to move him away from the tree and lay his head on the ground, screaming at him. This time I got the gurgling sounds of the word 'Simon'. He was conscious and breathing, but only just.

I knew he was in trouble but tried to make him comfortable. I started talking to him and he talked back to me the best he could through a terrible gargling voice. I cupped his head in my arms and he summoned me closer and asked me to tell his fiancée that he loved her. I assured him that I definitely would. With that he just looked at me blankly; by then he was a ghastly colour, the colour of death, I call it. He lost consciousness and stopped breathing so I began cardiac massage. I reached down to pump his chest but it felt like just soft pulp under my hands; it had all caved in from the impact with the tree, so I stopped. It was useless. I'll never forget how badly smashed up he was and still can't fathom how he managed to talk at all.

Then he died in my arms. Those few moments are still very clear and precise in my mind, and they come back every now and then as part of a nightmare that is so real, even more than two decades later. I have wondered ever since that day whether I could have saved his life if I had reacted quicker or better. What if I had got there earlier, kept working on him harder?

People started milling around. I had the situation under as much control as I could and stayed with Simon until the ambulance officers arrived and took him away. The driver of Simon's car only had a broken thumb and the driver of the van walked away without a scratch. Simon, an innocent passenger, died – probably because he wasn't wearing a seatbelt.

Straight afterwards I felt totally stuffed, emotionally and physically, like I'd gone ten rounds with Muhammad Ali. I was twenty-one and this was my first hands-on experience with a bad traffic accident. I had never seen someone die, and it had a marked affect on my psyche. Because I was a soldier I thought I should have been able to handle the situation and that I should have been able to just get on with life as normal. I was in complete denial, thinking there was nothing wrong with me. I should have sought help but, hey, I was a trained soldier, supposed to be strong enough to cope with disaster. 'Don't be such a sook.'

I went to see Simon's fiancée – I think I got her details off his mate in the car – and nearly dropped dead when I found she was very pregnant with their first child. I passed on Simon's dying words and watched the tears run down her face – I will never forget her sad face – then offered my condolences and walked away to get on with my life, knowing hers had been ruined. It was years later, when the nightmares of that scene were driving me crazy, before I admitted to Tracey that Simon had died in my arms. I'd told her he was still alive when I left him and he died in the ambulance. It was my way of protecting her from the ordeal and I think it also shielded me from the gravity of the situation, not having to explain it to someone else.

Unbelievably, less than two weeks later I was at home with a few mates while Tracey was away at her mother's in Geraldton when I heard the same deathly sound again. This time a young guy had gone through the stop sign in his car and straight into a tree. He was dead by the time I got to him. I looked inside the car and felt physically ill at the ghastly sight. The driver was in an awful fucking mess; he'd virtually been ripped open like a watermelon right down his head to his neck. I couldn't find a pulse; he was dead as a door nail. As soon as I realised he was gone I had to get out of there – I just couldn't cope. I made a hasty retreat home.

These two events contributed more than anything, I believe, towards the years of mental torture I later put myself through. In those days there was little knowledge of how to treat such psychological trauma, nor was I aware of any sort of avenue where I could seek treatment for the grief I carried inside from those events. Alongside this were physical injuries I also suffered while in the army which, in the end, couldn't wait to spit me out of its system. I needed expert help, but I was in denial and didn't go looking for any, thinking that as a soldier I should be able to handle my mental issues myself – plus there was such a stigma associated with mental illness I just thought I could soldier on and keep it all inside.

Those terrible car accidents happened in 1987 and soon after that I started to drink more to try to escape from the anguish they caused me. And when I had a few drinks I could fly off the handle too easily, which contributed towards me being court martialled the next year for assaulting a fellow sapper who, I'd been told, had just called my wife a slut.

I can't remember it at all but in the evidence he gave at my court martial hearing, he said I confronted him on the way from the Sportsman's Club (the army bar) to our barracks after we'd been to a formal dinner and had a few drinks afterwards. I apparently said if he had anything to say to me he should say it to my face and not behind my back, and when he snapped, 'What's up with you, Paterson?' I tried to hit him with my right fist but he grabbed it. I then threw a left fist at him which he also grabbed, which suggests how drunk I must have been. So I did what anyone would have done in that situation – I head-butted him! Now let me tell you the whole story: I was the fifth and last one to hit the drunken dickhead, who annoyed the hell out of everyone that night, but I was the only one to cop a court martial – supposedly because I was the only one who opened him up (caused a cut). The other four were charged with assault and had their pays docked; I copped fourteen days confined to barracks and a twelve-month suspended jail sentence – I reckon purely because the commanding officer didn't like me.

Further upset was just around the corner. In July 1989 I was packet commander (in charge of six vehicles) on the way to training operations in the Northern Territory near Katherine. We had an accident on the way up when an MKV petrol tanker hit one of our trucks which had pulled up on the wrong side of it, with me standing alongside it; it missed me by inches. It meant a 200-kilometre detour to take one of our men to hospital with a broken ankle. Later during this exercise I also started suffering really bad headaches for the first time, and was sent back to Perth to hospital for a few days. I was diagnosed with neuralgia. I begged to be returned to K89 (the name of the training exercise) and fortunately I was sent back via a supply plane which had to stop over at Richmond RAAF Base (and just about every other base in Australia while travelling on the 'milk run'; it was like cattle-class), which allowed me to see my parents for a short while. Mum looked really good, really full of life; she was so happy to see me and seemed really contented. I thought, 'Great, maybe she has cleaned herself out,' (I have a great last photo of the family together taken that day) but I never got to see her in such a good state again. That was the last time I saw my mother alive.

Weeks later, on Sunday 13 August, we were supposed to have a day off and go to Mataranka Springs. However, the Kamarians (the name given to the enemy in the exercise) were in our area of operations and the siren sounded to signal us to go into battle mode. It was a regimental exercise so there were well over 2000 soldiers involved, plus the navy and air force, in what was the biggest military exercise the army undertook in those days. We all went into the gun pits and fighting bays and stayed there for nearly an hour but as it turned out it must have been a false identification of the enemy and the battle was postponed.

We were told we could have local leave for three hours, so we went into Katherine to have a few beers. When we got back I was told to report immediately to the squadron commander at the command post and I naturally thought, 'What have I done this time?' The commanding officer told me to call my wife urgently. When I got on the phone Tracey told me my mother had died; she was just forty-two! I was overwhelmed with grief and felt like my whole world had turned upside down. I was hysterical and inconsolable. It was later that the coroner's report put it down to congestive cardiac failure, a heart attack; but I thought she might have got some pills and taken the dosage she used to previously and, because she had been clean for a while and her body wasn't used to it, that contributed to the heart failing. We'll never know for sure. What broke my heart was that she looked so good when I saw her, and seemed to have kicked the habit, and I knew she loved her grandson so much and was so happy when we told her just a few weeks earlier that Tracey was pregnant again.

They got the padre to comfort me and, you wouldn't believe it, the only night we saw any action from the Kamarians happened that evening while I was sitting in a bunker with the padre – a full-scale assault taking place outside. I could hear the sounds of gunfire, mortar simulations, flares and all the other stuff. It felt surreal. In hindsight it feels bizarre that this was the only attack against the camp in the whole five-month exercise. I certainly won't forget that terrible night.

I was grieving badly, which led to my squadron quartermaster sergeant telling me to wake up to myself and that I should have expected it. I'd confided in him earlier about Mum's drug problem. I just wanted to kill the insensitive bastard, but luckily my mates were there to stop me. He really hurt me. Looking back, he was an alcoholic and had no compassion in his body, but to me it was just another example of the coldness of the army.

As I said, just before my mother died we learned that Tracey was pregnant again, and on 29 March 1990 Karah came into the world. It was wonderful to have a healthy baby girl and she was just beautiful and such a joy. The perception of us tough Aussie blokes is that we all yearn for a boy to teach footy to and have a beer with when they 'come of age', but I tell you I got just as big a buzz out of having a daughter, and I have been proud of her ever since, as I have with our second lovely girl, Krystal.

Soon after, I was posted to 20 Divisional Engineer Support Squadron at Enoggera in Brisbane, where the shit hit the fan on two counts. We were there only a few weeks when I called my father and he relayed to me that my cousin Roy had committed suicide; he'd driven to a hill outside of Mittagong and put a hose from the exhaust pipe into his car. Roy was a bit older than me and had also been in the army but got himself out, for reasons I can't remember. But he was just a lost soul out of uniform and had applied to re-enlist, which you could do in the first twelve months after your discharge. The day he killed himself a letter arrived saying he'd been accepted back in, but he never knew it. Bloody tragic. That shocked me enough but when I asked Dad when it had happened he said on 20 July – my birthday! I felt guilty enough because I had encouraged Roy to go into the army in the first place, telling him what a great life it was.

A few months after that I badly hurt my knee playing Australian football in the army. I'd been having a bit of a run-in with one of the opponents, a physical instructor from the infantry unit, and he 'took me out' from the side as I took a mark; my knee just collapsed under me. It was diagnosed as a partial tear of the anterior cruciate ligament and a bucket-handle tear of the meniscus and I was told to rest for a while and that it would then be okay. Bullshit. It was agony for some time and that's when I was put on regular painkillers and found they gave me relief, physically and mentally. Eventually I had to have a complete reconstruction but that wasn't diagnosed until three years later. It wasn't much fun in the meantime, especially when I also had recurring problems with my back.

Most of 1991 and 1992 is a blur to me, other than the birth of Krystal on 5 February 1992 – ah, another beautiful little girl coming into the Paterson family. I'd become hooked on injecting painkillers. I started 'doctor shopping' and smoking cannabis too. Doctor shopping is where you go from doctor to doctor to secure prescriptions. Few doctors' surgeries were on computer back then and thus they didn't know if I had sought drugs somewhere else, so it wasn't hard to get a pretty constant supply – particularly when I went into surgeries in my army uniform telling them how much pain I was in, which I often was. The thing that shames me most to admit is that at my worst, while in Brisbane, I actually broke into a doctor's surgery one night in a desperate search for drugs – something I would never even have contemplated doing with a straight mind. It just shows how the power of addiction can overrule any sane, rational thinking.

Somehow I had no trouble applying myself at work and staying 'straight', and I really loved coaching Cory in his rugby league teams too. When I had something to get my teeth into and feel rewarded from, I was okay, but when I had time on my hands and wasn't active, it was as if I had to escape from my life – even though I loved Tracey and the kids, and seeing our children grow up. I can't explain what it was but I seemed forever in pain, either from my bad knee or back, or from the headaches or from the nightmares of Simon and the other bloke who died in front of me, and the only way to numb myself from those things was to get drunk or zap myself out on morphine or pethidine.

We were posted from Brisbane to Canberra in December 1992 and the year we spent there was terrible. I was posted to a really mundane storeman's position in an office where there were no windows. I hated it. I didn't get on with some of the people I worked with and went off the rails even more. Tracey obviously had just about had enough of me and I couldn't, or wouldn't, try to get things off my mind and spill them out to her or anyone else. Soldiers are supposed to handle their problems, right?

On Christmas Day I injured my back again when trying to move boxes at our new posting. The ambulance came and took me to hospital; they gave me a shot of pethidine and sent me home in a taxi. A couple of days later I was in hospital again. I'd been having trouble sleeping for some time by then and I'd break out in a cold sweat and have flashbacks about the accidents. I thought I was going fucking crazy, so I saw the medical officer at the RAP (regimental aid post) at Duntroon in Canberra. She was fantastic. She thought I might have been suffering from post-traumatic stress disorder and sent me to a psychiatrist – finally, someone got me to talk about my demons. But that treatment ended when my job in Canberra became redundant and I was posted to the School of Military Engineering at Holsworthy, in Sydney's south-west. The posting in Canberra didn't leave me with too many good memories; I also suffered pneumonia while there and ended up in hospital yet again for a few days.

I wasn't much better in the head while we were in Sydney either, due to a series of events: administering first aid to a bloke who was in a pretty bad way after falling out of his truck (I was given a commendation for my 'professionalism and compassion' in dealing with an accident victim); raging bushfires not far from the base; doing my knee badly again while playing touch football; and finally getting the right diagnosis that I needed a knee reconstruction – all within the first year in Sydney.

I can't believe it took three years of pain and telling the authorities something was seriously wrong with my knee before someone finally realised my knee was fucked. But, surprise surprise, I had complications after the operation. Tracey and I had made arrangements to go home to Western Australia for Christmas with her family. She asked the surgeon if I would be right to travel (I had the operation in early November) so she could book the airfares. He said he couldn't see any problems at all and that I'd only be in hospital for five days. Bullshit! It was seventeen days later before I was released. The leg swelled badly and I was in a lot of pain but the doctor kept saying there was nothing wrong and it was just sore from the surgery. Eventually the physiotherapist almost got him in a headlock and said, 'Mate, there is definitely something wrong with his leg – I reckon he's got deep vein thrombosis, his leg is hot and swollen.' He was absolutely right. I was put on the anticoagulant Warfarin and it was also suspected I had septic arthritis, although this was never confirmed.

We were keen to get back to Western Australia for Christmas and I was told I would be fine to travel by plane, as ridiculous as that sounds now. Within thirty-six hours of flying into Geraldton I was back in hospital with a knee as big as my head. During the week I spent in the Geraldton hospital I had my knee drained twice. The medication wasn't working so the doctors decided the best course of action was to fly me 500 kilometres to Perth for more treatment. I was taken by the Flying Doctor Service for another operation and was in hospital for two more weeks, missing Christmas with the family, New Year's Eve and our ninth wedding anniversary. They finally stabilised my leg and sent me back to Geraldton to continue my leave.

In March 1995 I wrote a letter of complaint about my treatment to the commanding officer of the field hospital. The doctor had failed to diagnose the DVT and I felt I had been labelled a narcotic abuser and made to feel it was entirely my fault. The army avoided any portion of the blame. My life was changed dramatically by what I have always regarded as maltreatment but I didn't have a leg to stand on, excuse the pun. If I had been treated properly in the first place and didn't need so much constant pain relief, well, who knows …?

At this stage I felt my life just absolutely sucked, and it all came to a head one night when I decided to ride my pushbike home from the Corporals Club and got clipped by a car along Moorebank Avenue, Moorebank. I was sent tumbling on my arse and had a heap of skin taken from me. It really rocked me; I thought, 'Fuck it, can life get any worse?' When I got home I went straight to the shower and got some razor blades and I began cutting both my wrists. Tracey knew it was out of character for me to go straight to the shower – usually I just sank onto the lounge –

and she sensed something was up. She barged into the bathroom and asked what was going on. I said, 'Nothing,' but she knew better and told me to show her what was behind my back. When I did she saw I'd cut my wrist and started screaming at me and took the razor from me. I really think it was more a cry for help than a genuine attempt to take my life. It was a bloody stupid thing to do, especially at home with the kids in the house. Tracey bandaged my arms but was incredibly angry and told me to contact the army medical people and do something about my life – she'd had enough of living on the edge with a human time bomb.

That night I had the duty officer come and pick me up and he called the medical officer who referred me to a psychologist at Concord Hospital. During my admission to Concord I began seeing Major Monica Kleinmann. She too was great; we talked about the accidents and touched on the pethidine use and how I'd had so much of it over the years, all due to injuries. I was admitted to the Concord Repatriation Hospital's psychiatric ward where I spent ten days. After I was released I kept visiting Monica at Randwick for a couple of months and we talked a lot about the accidents and the two men dying and it definitely eased my pain, but I arrived for my appointment one day only to be told it had been cancelled – by the army. No one had had the decency to tell me! It was deemed I'd been reporting well for my duties and that I was virtually cured. It was the furthest thing from the truth.

After a honeymoon period of a few months I began to doctor shop again. I was getting increasingly depressed and drinking and drugging nearly every day. I felt I was going off my head. Tracey and I were really struggling with my inner demons and our relationship was affected worse than ever. I knew I had to try to do something before I killed myself or hurt my family even more – I was so impatient and intolerant when I was in pain or just spaced out when I sought relief in the drugs. I was told to speak to Army Community Services. They virtually said, however, that under army policy they couldn't help me if I had a drug problem but if I had an alcohol problem they could, so I had to exaggerate how much and how often I drank to get some treatment.

In 1996 I was sent to the Army Rehabilitation and Education Program (AREP) at Richmond RAAF Base where I really tried hard to get myself back on track again. Not for the army, not for my family, but for the most important person – me: Donny Paterson. AREP was a live-in course specifically developed for alcoholics. I guess one could say what's the difference, drug addiction or alcohol addiction? Well, it worried me that I had to admit to alcoholism as opposed to addiction to prescription drugs; I probably felt drug addicts thought differently to 'alkies'. I had to attend group therapy every day; some of the stuff was hard to deal with but I found it helpful in that there were others in the same sort of a predicament as me. At the end of the day, we were all fighting for our lives and our sanity, so labels really didn't matter, I suppose. As part of the program we had to write our own autobiographies. That was really difficult for me because I'd had so many moves as a kid. The only way that I could get it chronologically correct, or near as, was to ask my father to visit and we worked out that we had moved thirty times before I was seventeen. I moved many more times in the next 25-odd years too.

While in AREP I was again diagnosed as suffering from post-traumatic stress disorder but with depression this time as well. As part of the course Tracey had to join me for two weeks, and the three kids spent the last week living with me (while they attended a local school) and were also interviewed by the doctors and counsellors and told of my problems. Addiction affects an entire family and Tracey would come to group sessions with me and other families. I can genuinely say the seven weeks at AREP did me a world of good and introduced me to the twelve steps towards sobriety – daily goals towards staying sober – but it didn't cure me.

I'd requested a transfer some time earlier so we could go back to Perth and as it turned out just weeks after getting out of AREP I was sent to the other side of the country, but that proved a very bad mistake. There was no follow-up from the army on how I was progressing with my rehabilitation; the issue just seemed to be dropped and I was left to deal with it myself.

Life went from another 'honeymoon' to another crash and another charade of telling Tracey I was going to the gym or somewhere else when I'd be off on a doctor's surgery run, pathetically chasing a 'hit' of morphine or pethidine-based medication. I found it easier to get pethidine from a doctor than a beer at happy hour at a crowded bar. One particular doctor prescribed five ampoules of pethidine; two of them were injected while I was in the surgery and he gave me the other three to take home. I had built up such a resistance to pethidine that I was getting happy on quantities that would have knocked other people out or even killed them.

I'd gotten in so deep this time I felt scared, frustrated and alone because I had to hide and lie about my problem, especially to Tracey. It was something which I am still so remorsefully ashamed of. I can't explain the disgrace I felt; I knew it was out of character for the 'real' Donny Paterson, who I always believed was honest and caring and wanted so much to be a good husband, father and citizen; but the pethidine grabbed such a strong hold of me it turned me into someone else. I had this sense that when I was on duty or coaching the kids at footy, I had to stay focused, clean and responsible; when I was occupied and had some purpose or duty, I was fine. It was only when I was away from those sorts of responsibilities that I just went over the edge and felt I had to escape.

Early in 1997, when Cory was nearly ten, Karah seven and Krystal five, Tracey kicked me out. She just couldn't handle it anymore. I don't remember any of this because I was drunk, but Tracey tells how I went home and was bashing on the door. She called the army and I was taken back to the barracks in a paddy wagon. We were separated for a month. I lived at the barracks in Fremantle, but I found an excuse to go over and see Tracey and the kids as often as I could.

In the depths of my despair I took an overdose of pills but again I reckon it was as much a 'Will someone please take notice of me?' plea as a real attempt to end it all; well, that's what I believe now.

I spoke in confidence with my squadron sergeant major and told him I still had a drug problem. I was admitted to the psychiatric section of Perth's Hollywood Hospital where I spent two and a half months, and finally, finally, I was treated extensively for post-traumatic stress disorder. By this stage I felt no one in the unit wanted anything to do with me, that they saw me as just a druggie or a drunk and a crazy man. The exception was Warrant Officer 1 Mick Ryan, now retired, who came and visited me in hospital; he was the only one who held any hope for me and stuck by me. I can't begin to explain how grateful I was for his compassion. I appreciated so much just the fact that he took time to visit me, as no one else from my army 'mates' did. Without his support it might have been a different result.

If you have traumatic experiences while in battle I'd imagine the army has great resources to debrief you and help you deal with it, and your mates would empathise with you, but in peace time it seemed they didn't understand or didn't care enough. Maybe some of my mates were just ignorant about the sort of psychological problems that caused people to get hooked on drugs, but I'm sure many of them just thought 'Pato' was a no-hope drunk and druggie, which was really disappointing; I needed support from my mates. But then again, I must admit I had a similar attitude towards my mother, so I can't be too condemning of them – but it did leave me with a feeling that the 'esprit de corps' that had been rammed down my throat over the years was a load of crap.

The psychiatrist's name was Patterson, curiously, and when I was at my lowest ebb he asked me if I wanted to leave the army or stay on. I said, 'No, fuck the army.' If he'd asked me further into the treatment when I was on the improve, I might have answered differently, but that was it: I got my discharge papers while still in Hollywood. They didn't even wait until I was clear-minded and could make a considered decision; instead they went by what I had told that fucking doctor when I was in the depths of my despair. It was like they were looking for an easy way to get rid of an army problem child who was an embarrassment to the system. I didn't really think he was asking me officially if I wanted a discharge; there was no follow-up discussion like, 'Now, soldier, are you sure?' I felt it was a bit deceitful. When I saw the discharge papers I couldn't believe it. I thought, 'This is the job I was born to do and they are taking it away from me.' I'm not sure whether I could have fought the decision or not, but the fact was I didn't have the energy or clarity of mind to take the army on – I was just battling to get through each day. I feel the army failed in their duty of care; they failed me. I still miss the challenges, the variety, some of the people and wearing the uniform, which gave me a sense of pride each day.

I finished my treatment a few weeks later and was given three days to turn into a civilian. Yep, a whole three-day 'resettlement training' program which consisted of how to write a resumé and how to present yourself for a job, but few other skills and no counselling. I thought at least I would get a reasonable pension, but I got a pittance – plus the bill for the balance owed on the Land Rover I crashed back in 1987, which was over $2000. I had suffered knee injuries while participating in organised sport in the army; I had no psychological support after witnessing the two deaths from the car accidents (although I was partly responsible for that by not opening up to anyone, but then again my immediate superiors were aware of what I had gone through and didn't offer any guidance); I'd had band-aid treatment for my ongoing drug problem, and for that I was pigeon-holed as a drug addict and spat out as a bad taste.

It's obvious I have bitter memories of the army, memories which nearly destroyed me. But they are mostly about how my illness and issues were treated. I had some great times there. I have no regrets about joining up and wish I was still wearing a uniform and working as a field engineer. It's still a case of unfulfilled business in that I never saw the active service that I trained for, but finally I have learned to live with it and a lot of the bitterness is gone. I met some very good people in the services and it *is* a good life generally – if you don't fuck up or get badly injured.

I felt the army should have compensated me far better than they did initially, and thankfully a wonderful lady named Patricia Rowlands from the RSL's pensions department in Perth made us aware of our rights and entitlements and what process I needed to go through. After nearly a year – a tough year when Tracey worked her arse off as the major breadwinner – of filling in application forms, pleading my case and going through red tape, thanks to Patricia's help I was given a Totally and Permanently Incapacitated Pension, which I still receive today. That helped the bank balance, but I was to struggle with life outside of the army more than I did when I was in uniform.

4

CIVILIAN LIFE

Without the army, I plunged into a real depression. I felt like a worthless, defeated person with nothing to look forward to when in fact I had what a lot of young men would love to have – a wonderful wife and three healthy and happy children. Tracey says it was like someone had run over me, reversed back and done it again. She says I became really meek and mild and submissive. I went from anger at the army for abandoning me to drowning myself in self-pity. It was a dark time in my life; I was on the brink. Sure, I was happy to have more time to see the kids grow up, but I had so much resentment built up inside of me. And money was bloody tight with only Tracey's wage and my mere part-pension coming in for a while. I was in a pit of depression.

As I was doctor shopping in the first months as a civilian, I came across the GP Dr Brett Christmas, who I believe saved my life. He wasn't fooled when I used the chronic back and knee pain as a reason for the painkillers. He saw through that and wanted to address the cause of my dependence. Not that I wasn't in pain – I was pretty much all the time and I needed relief – but I just exaggerated the pain to get higher dosages of medication. Brett treated me in a very nonjudgmental way, though, and he was the first person to prescibe me antidepressive medication. He was also the first person I felt understood what was going on inside of me and that I needed help for the causes of my problems, not the symptoms, and for that I am eternally grateful.

Another saving grace was the South Perth Rugby League Club where I coached Cory's team and became the first-aid trainer for the whole junior club. It was my release, where I felt appreciated. On Saturdays and Sundays I could occupy myself with something that was purposeful and rewarding. And it was something that brought Cory and me back together; whether I had chastised him, or been on a bender or was impatient and snappy, we loved being involved in footy together from when he started playing at age five until he was into his teens and my knees were so bad I couldn't kick the ball with him anymore without pain and I thought I should step back from Cory's football and let someone else coach him.

Tracey hated how I lived my life. She'd just lost her brother Steven to cancer at age twenty-eight, not long after he and his wife had had a son, and here I was wallowing in self-pity. God, it hurts to think back on those times and how I stung and disappointed my family. I can't take any of that back but I can, and have definitely tried to, make up for it and tried to use my experiences to inspire others. I broke the behaviour; I feel full of life and worth now, even though I have two crook knees and have to take antidepressants for the rest of my life. There are a whole lot of people worse off than me; I've seen a lot of them, and I have some great things happening in my life now. But for the sake of telling my whole story, I have to confess to so many wasted years in civilian clothes.

In September 1997, just a few months after my discharge, I became one of the first people in Australia to try naltrexone treatment. Naltrexone is described as an opiate antagonist which stops addicts 'feeling high'. Perth obstetrician George O'Neil had been using it since June that year to treat his patients who were heroin addicts. I'd been on a methadone program since February that year and had to go through methadone withdrawal for two weeks before starting the naltrexone, and that was tough. It was a pretty controversial treatment at the time and I was the subject of a newspaper article in the *West Australian* (using my Christian name only) about the treatment and the West Australian government's consideration of whether to allow it to continue. It is interesting to look back on the article now. I was quoted as saying: 'We are not all criminals; we don't live in seedy back alleys shooting up. We are normal people who come from normal healthy families.' So that year I had six and a half months on methadone and about three months on naltrexone, but the naltrexone wasn't as successful as I would have liked so I didn't continue with it.

During the period 1998 to 2001, I admitted myself into Niola Private Hospital, a psychiatric hospital in Perth, five times, staying several weeks at a time. After coming out I would be straight for a while and feel a better person, but I would always head back to my old ways of escaping from real life, and from the mental and physical pain that sometimes consumed me. It was a hell of a time.

A low point came in 2001 when Tracey rang the hospital to see if I needed any clothes, only to find I'd discharged myself. I'd blown up because one of the patients was smuggling marijuana into the clinic, which I thought wasn't right. They let me walk out with ten 100mg tablets of morphine; I was supposed to use 300mg of morphine a day as 'maintenance'. That's a lot of morphine, but for me that was a reduced amount to what I could easily tolerate, a quantity meant to wean me off it. I went around the corner and took half of them. Then there was the time Tracey followed me in the car when she saw me walking along the street one day; she found me at the back of a toilet block injecting myself. She saw red and said that after all the years of trying to support me and see me get through my troubles, she was out of my life. I'd lost the thing most special to me – my wife and three children.

I roamed the streets for days thinking about how my life could have sunk to this level, and I slept on the street of a night. I rang Tracey to see if I could go home, promising her I'd sort myself out, but those words were understandably sounding hollow by then and she said I was not welcome. Another wonderful woman from Military Compensation and Rehabilitation, Angela Piesley, found out about my plight and bent over backwards to help me find some temporary accommodation and gave me money for food; I was very grateful to her.

So I checked into Perth Clinic as a last hope of straightening myself out. Perth Clinic in West Perth is a wonderful place that specialises in psychiatric problems, from mood disorders, post-natal depression, post-traumatic stress, anxiety and panic behaviour to alcohol and drug abuse and other conditions. Someone at Niola had said it was a good place to go to and the decision to follow that recommendation ended up being the turning point in my life, to a degree – but not until I reached the bottom. I think it's absolutely correct that when you suffer depression or terrible personal problems like I did, you have to reach your rock bottom before you can get on a sustained journey back up.

I didn't know how to face Tracey so I called her mother, who was then living in Perth, and asked her would she mind going to my place and getting some clothes and dropping them in to me at the clinic. Apparently Tracey said she would save her mum the trouble and drop the clothes in herself. She brought them to the front reception, but when asked if she wanted to see me, she told the woman at the desk that she didn't. I think the woman called through and I walked out the front to collect the clothes and saw the back of Tracey walking out the door. That shattered me. My own wife had come to the clinic but didn't want to see me, didn't want to know me. That was my rock bottom. I thought I had nothing to live for. I might never have any reasonable relationship with my family or, at the worst, might never even see them again. I could react by either doing something about my life or ending it.

Another really hurtful moment was when Cory, who was fourteen, refused to visit me. He didn't want to have a bar of his old man. I'd obviously hurt him so much, and that hurt me; he felt I'd betrayed him or didn't care for him, which was absolutely incorrect. Karah and Krystal would visit, but Tracey would drop them off and wait outside for them. After quite a few weeks the feedback Tracey received from the kids and the doctors made her aware that I'd finally started to become stronger, more positive, and I was genuinely insistent this time that I was going to do something about my life. Slowly I was able to reconcile with my family and some friends. About then my old army mate Mick Ryan came in and had a good chat to me; to have someone who thought I was worth sticking by really lifted my spirits. Mick had no idea how that hour spent with me helped me on my road to recovery.

Doctors at Perth Clinic diagnosed me as suffering from clinical depression and were the first to treat it other than just providing medication like what Dr Christmas had put me on. I had a psychiatrist who I was really happy with, Dr Steve Proud, and a real breakthrough was undergoing cognitive behaviour therapy (CBT): I referred to it as 'combat training'. The basis of the treatment is that when you get a negative thought, try to challenge it. I'll steal a few lines from Perth Clinic's website to explain CBT, because I think it is an important development in psychiatric treatment.

> **Cognition is a broad term which refers to the way a person interprets situations, as well as thoughts, images and attitudes. Basically, the way a person thinks about or interprets an event affects their mood and their behaviour. A person can alter the**

way he or she feels and behaves by altering the way they interpret the situation ... it refers to the person closely examining his interpretation to see if it is based in reality or is a self-defeating way of looking at life. As an example, a very stressed and anxious person walking down the corridor at work sees one of his managers who passes without smiling. He immediately thinks he must have done something wrong or perhaps he isn't working hard enough. This reinforces his belief that he is not good at his job and that he must work harder, which causes him to become even more stressed and anxious, which in turn reduces his ability to perform well. There is no evidence for this belief – there are many different interpretations. For instance, the manager may be pre-occupied, worrying about a meeting with their own boss, or thinking about a problem at home. During therapy, much focus is placed upon learning to challenge such negative, irrational and self-defeating thoughts.

Behavioural strategies are also important to help people suffering depression. These people often begin to withdraw from activities that once

were sources of pleasure as they often become lethargic and exhausted. By encouraging the person to slowly recommence pleasurable and self-nurturing activities, slowly their mood begins to improve.

One of my most pleasurable activities was being involved in the rugby league club and Cory's football, so I ploughed my energies into that and it was really helpful and therapeutic. I began to connect with Cory again, and became closer to Karah and Krystal. But outside of that, I still suffered from lack of motivation and purpose because I had so many hours to fill in while everyone else was at school or work. I couldn't work because of the pain in my knees, and the constant battle with my psychological issues, and my army pension allows me to work only eight hours a week in any case. I'd go to footy training on Tuesdays and Thursdays, and be at the juniors' games on Saturday and the seniors on Sunday doing the first aid; I'm sure everyone saw me as energetic, outgoing Donny.

At football I was occupied, I was respected and appreciated, and that made me feel great. But away from that I was still depressed, despite taking medication daily, and retreated within myself. I tried to follow all the CBT principles, and it certainly helped, as I never got back into doctor shopping again and only take painkillers under strict medical guidance and usually only when in hospital. And I've stuck to that ever since. The nightmares about Simon and the victim of the other fatal accident became less regular, as did the headaches. I was a better person, that's for sure, but not the person I could be. I also had to have surgery on my other knee, as its cruciate ligament was also shot, and had a full knee replacement on my bad knee in October 2008.

We bought our own house in Parkwood in 1999 and I enjoyed some part-time work too, guiding a few camping trips around Perth and sometimes to the outback for an outback adventure tour company. I'd take small groups and be in charge of setting up camp, cooking and showing them the sights – which was great, although very demanding. However, rugby league was my great outlet and it was pleasing to see that Cory was able to develop so well that he was given an opportunity to play for the National Rugby League team the Newcastle Knights. His football journey began back in 1992 when he played in the under 7s, even though he was only five, at West Mitchelton, the same club that Paul 'Fatty' Vautin and Michael Hagan played at when they were kids. I coached his team then and when we moved to Canberra I coached his under-6 side at the South Tuggeranong Knights. That's when Cory really began to shine – over fifty tries one season and having his picture on the front page of the local paper with a big write-up, and also featuring in the Canberra Raiders' club magazine. It was while I was posted in Canberra that I did my level 1 coaching certificate. Later I did my sports trainers and senior first-aid certificates. I also played touch football before my knees were no good and represented at state level in the army as well as getting my level 3 refereeing certificate; I loved touch footy.

After we moved to Sydney when Cory was seven, he won Canterbury–Bankstown junior player of the year out of 800 players, while playing for the Moorebank Rams. I probably went over the top in how I reacted, but I was so proud of him and I was his coach as well as his father. It was a great achievement and made us both realise he had the talent to do something as a rugby league player if he wanted to. He loved goalkicking too, so I got some PVC pipes and made goal posts for our backyard and he would bang the ball over them from all directions. I loved those times together.

Fortunately Cory wanted to keep playing rugby league when we went back to Perth, even though it is an avid Australian football city. And he is fortunate to be one of the few players scouted from Perth to make it all the way to the National Rugby League. That became possible after he performed well with the West Australian schoolboys side in Sydney in 2002. The Knights development manager, Warren Smiles, was impressed and put him on a 'gear scholarship', which basically meant he got some boots and a club jersey and was officially under notice by the Knights.

The following year Cory again competed in the Australian schoolboys championships. Warren Smiles was impressed by how much Cory had developed physically and performance-wise in the twelve months between the two championships. Cory had just missed out on being selected in the Australian Institute of Sport rugby league program based in Canberra so he asked Tracey and me if he could ring Warren and ask him if he could go to Newcastle to trial with the Knights. It was September 2003 and he was only sixteen but he was so focused and knew what he wanted. Warren agreed to allow him to trial but offered him no promises. So Tracey took Cory to Newcastle and it was purely coincidental that she sat next to Jarrod Mullen's mother, Leanne, in the grandstand during the trials. They got on exceptionally well and Tracey told Leanne how Cory was hoping to be selected and if he was he would move over to live in Newcastle to follow his dreams. Leanne offered to speak to her husband, Steve, about whether Cory could stay with their family. It was a wonderful gesture and Cory was fortunate to stay with Leanne and Steve Mullen's lovely family and attend the same school as Jarrod, St Francis Xavier College, which was a strong rugby league school. It's incredible to think they have both progressed to first grade together and are still the best of mates.

Jarrod and Cory played for a Newcastle team that won the SG Ball grand final that next season. Jarrod was a standout player of the future as he made the New South Wales under 17s and the Australian schoolboys team. Tracey and I flew to Sydney for the grand final played at a ground in St Marys. The Knights won 42–6 over South Sydney and Cory played off the interchange bench for the first time (he had started in other games). It was a great team performance; that Newcastle team included Jarrod, Kade Snowden, Terence Seuseu and Luke Walsh, who all went on to play first grade with Cory.

But as the year went on it was obvious Cory would be better off having his family around him. He was homesick and we missed him heaps too. Tracey and I went over a couple of times during the year while Cory came home in the school holidays. Another time we brought the girls and rented a house for a few weeks and we were all able to be back as one family unit. I think it was affecting Cory's football having such instability, although we couldn't have wished for him to have a better place to stay or better people to stay with than the Mullen family. So in October 2004 we packed up and left Perth to make Newcastle our home. Packing all our stuff into a six-metre container and relocating wasn't new to us – we'd got the process down pat – but it wasn't easy leaving friends and the South Perth footy club, and for the girls to change schools and

Mum and Dad in happier times.

A cheerful moment with my estranged dad.

Life was tough at Kapooka; here we clean up after a 16-kilometre battle efficiency test.

Tracey and I tie the knot in January 1987: a great day.

Author's collection

One of the earliest shots of Tracey, baby Cory and me.

Author's collection

Cory (with the ball) playing for the Newcastle Knights. It has been very rewarding to see him achieve his footy dreams.

Newspix 719830 (photo: Greg Porteous)

Above and below: we were greeted with absolute devastation at Peraliya.

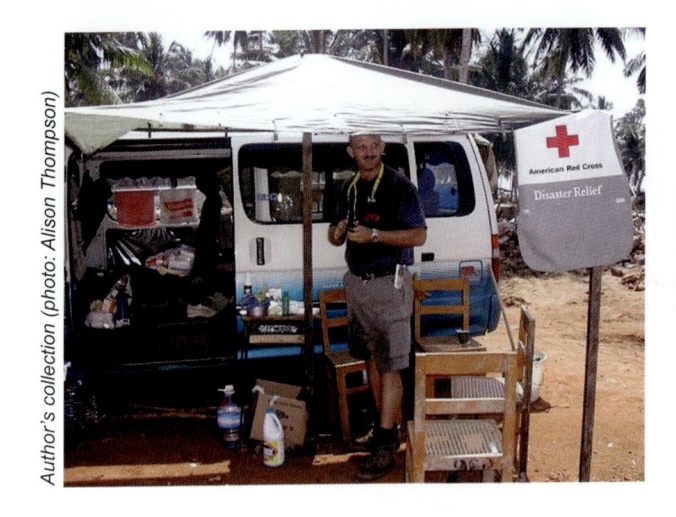

Day one at Peraliya: a temporary first-aid station set up under my hoochie at the side of our hired van.

Author's collection (photo: Alison Thompson)

The 'Fab Four' – Bruce, Alison, Oscar and me.

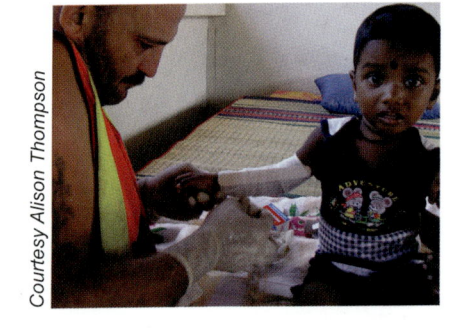

Courtesy Alison Thompson

'Second aid' medicos at work: Alison and I attending to the injured. Me bandaging the arm of a lovely wide-eyed girl (left); and (below) both of us removing splinters from a man who was washed inland by 'the wave'.

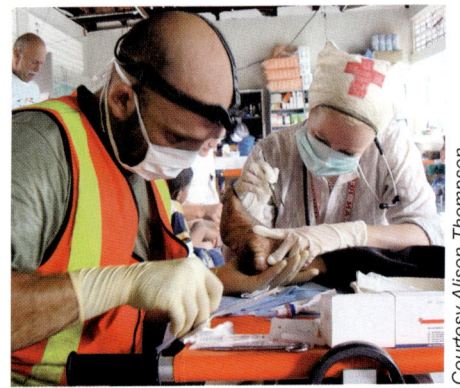

Courtesy Alison Thompson

Courtesy Alison Thompson

My first construction at Peraliya ... a slit trench for everyone to do their 'business' in.

Lined up for help. This shot shows some of the masses that came to the 'heart' of Peraliya for medical treatment.

The first temporary shelter – which appropriately went to the chief. He still uses it as a kitchen today.

The damaged *Queen of the Sea* back on the tracks at Peraliya.

Donny and Dinny: me standing with Dinesh along the main railway line in Peraliya.

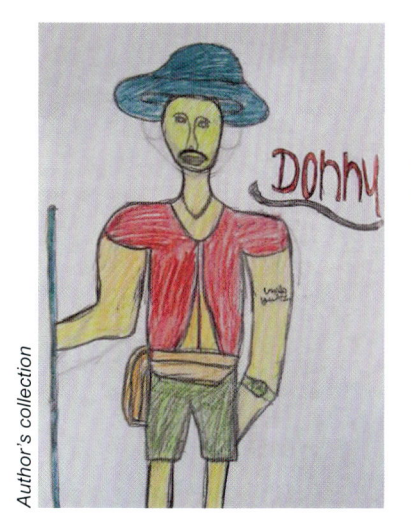

A picture of me drawn by one of the village children.

Author's collection

A prized souvenir. The chief's son made this carving from a photo which appeared in the *Observer* in Britain (pinned on the wall).

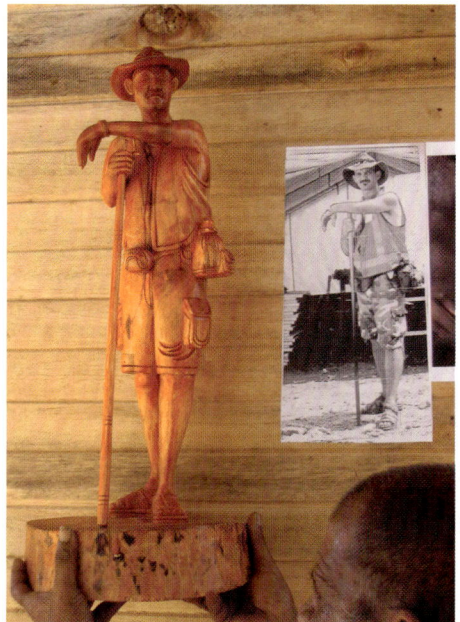

Courtesy Alison Thompson

With my flock ... the kids kept me going on the tough days.

Author's collection

The 'Fab Four' taking a break at Alluthawalla.

Courtesy Alison Thompson

This was our family portrait that Kumara superimposed his family onto. He, his wife, two children and sister are all dead now.

Author's collection

move the width of the continent. But as a family, it was something we wanted and needed to do.

Football has always been a family thing for us, and we've all supported Cory and still love to go to his matches together. Karah played rugby league when she was younger, too, and was very good. In Perth the missus and my two daughters played in a women's rugby league team that I coached. Tracey also served time on both the junior and women's committees and she ran the canteen at all junior home games. Karah and Krystal would often help out in the canteen or have some sort of duties while I did the first aid – it was a real family outing that we all enjoyed. That's one of the great things about rugby league.

We moved into a rented place at Lambton Gardens and we'd only been there less than three months when we had our first Christmas in Newcastle. I remember looking around the room on Christmas Day thinking that at least those days of doctor shopping and being 'Druggie Donny' were behind me, and I was happy that all the family was together again. But I wasn't fulfilled with my life. I knew there was something, or someone, inside me that could contribute a lot more than I was. But I'd long stopped searching inside of me trying to find that person. I was in the rut of just getting through each day with nothing urgent to do and nothing inspiring to attempt. I hadn't joined any sporting clubs at that stage (it was the rugby league off-season), knew hardly anyone outside of the family, and my life seemed to be restricted to the four walls of our rented house.

It took a real disaster to change my perceptions. Let's pick up the story again at Peraliya, and the people who would never complain about the restrictions of the four walls of their home – they didn't have any such luxury.

5

THE THIRD WAVE

Peraliya, 11 January 2005. A village that had lost 249 of its residents, a quarter or more of its population, and had 1643 more bodies from the *Queen of the Sea* train dumped on it by a watery Grim Reaper. When my fellow volunteers and I took an exit from the main Colombo-to-Galle road and entered the lives of those who'd survived, it was a village that had lost its main industry – fishing – just about every one of its buildings, and all its hope too. There were four of us who wanted to make a difference for a couple of weeks – somewhere, somehow. For Alison, Oscar, Bruce and me – all vastly different characters from different backgrounds – it became our 'workplace' and we couldn't stay just for the planned two weeks. Instead, for five months it was where we went through every possible emotion – despair, frustration, anger, helplessness, sadness, love, laughter, exhaustion, introspection, satisfaction but most of all, pride at what we achieved.

I'll never forget the sight that confronted us. Galle Road, the main thoroughfare from Colombo to Galle, looked like a street-sweeper had pushed the contents of a hundred rubbish tips to the sides of the bitumen. The train stood, a little mangled but largely intact, on the train tracks just metres from the edge of the road. In between I saw a child's shoe; it broke my heart to think of what might have happened to its owner. From there we walked to a clearing in the middle of the small village; rubble and rubbish were piled up everywhere. No matter what direction I looked in, it was the same – an obliterated, flattened and tangled wasteland. How could anyone have survived this? It seemed as though ninety-nine per cent of a once thriving fishing village had been steamrolled. And those expressionless, helpless faces looked at us as though they weren't capable of any emotion or even acknowledgment that we had arrived. As I said at the start of this book, they were zombies. They just sat, or stood, as if still in shock – and this was two and a half weeks after the tsunami had hit.

That was my initial sight. Then there was the sound, this pathetic wailing of women who had lost their families; some of them had seen their children washed from their clinging arms, taken by the monstrous wave or the wall of water that followed it and washed miles inland, never to be seen again.

The smell left the most overpowering impression. The putrid smell of decomposing flesh. That unmistakable odour is something which still haunts me today: the bloody rancid smell of death. I would never become used to that smell. It reached a point where I'd be gagging and dry-retching as I became more and more enveloped in this huge catastrophe. It was obvious we were in a place that had suffered immensely; it was written on the faces of the survivors. 'These poor bastards,' I thought. 'I can't begin to understand what they must have gone through.'

We walked into the village and asked the blank faces we met if anyone spoke English. We were fortunate that one of them, a young man in his early twenties called Chinthu, was a lieutenant in the Sri Lankan army, and spoke impeccable English. The rapport between us was instant after I established that I'd been in the Australian army. We asked him could we see the chief of the village and we were led to a grey-bearded man in his early sixties, I guessed, Aiyypyge Darmadasa. We said we had come of our own accord and asked him, through our newly appointed translator Chinthu, what we could do to help them; we were only a few but we'd come here to see what we could do. We said, 'Look, we have some bags of rice and some medical supplies,' and when the words 'medical supplies' got around the village, within half an hour the place was just swarming with people with cuts and bruises and injuries a whole lot worse.

The chief told us we were welcome. But where would we start? That question was answered quite easily in the finish: we started from the centre and worked our way out. The villagers were in no frame of mind to initiate a rebuilding of their town themselves; they were so obviously still grieving and most had lost all their possessions – house, vehicle, boat, clothing and self-respect as they were forced to live on the streets or under the carriages of the death-trap train. And they'd received virtually no outside help, or even interest. The millions of dollars that according to the news bulletins had flooded into the tsunami-affected countries certainly hadn't made their way to Peraliya, nor many other parts along the Galle Road, as we were to find out in the ensuing weeks. Even the Sri Lankan government had done little, other than have a work gang bulldoze a mass grave to get the bodies out of sight and away from the busy road.

Trucks, tuk-tuks and the odd car just drove straight past. Those who stopped did so to take a photo of the train, or to pray for loved ones lost when the train was hit by the two massive waves. The train became a macabre worship site. Visitors saw people starving and traumatised but did nothing. As I've said, that irked me so much in those first few days. I thought, 'Fuck me, they pause over the train and not one of 'em offers any help.

Are they blind to the serious need of these people?' How many people had died after the tsunami before we got there while others just passed by? How could people just visit and not offer any help? It still astounds me all these years later.

There was no fresh water in the village, and that was a major issue. There appeared to be little food, too, so we cooked rice and exhausted all our supplies in one day feeding hundreds and hundreds, thinking we would buy more the next day. Bruce, who was used to cooking the best organic food for the rich and famous, never had such a 'clientele' or as basic a menu. There were no toilets so people were doing their business anywhere on the streets or in the rubble, which caused a further health hazard. Most of the inhabitants sat on the ground in the day and slept on the same dirt at night because they had no homes.

We walked around the place as Chinthu explained what had happened, and it was easy to work out what needed doing first. People had injuries that needed urgent attention: broken limbs that required splints of some sort, wounds that needed stitching or cuts and grazes that needed disinfecting to avoid serious infection. We had to start somewhere so we put up a temporary shelter off our van – actually, it was my old army hootchie (a small waterproof tarpaulin to sleep under) – and we had a mobile first-aid station. All we could do was patch them up. We didn't have any drugs; Panadol was the strongest thing we had then, but it was better than the local remedies they were getting. A lot of the injured had just been patched up by applying their native treatments which they were used to using as part of the traditional Indian medicine called Ayurveda. So I called what we did 'second aid', actually. I don't know how many hundreds lined up in the next few hours. The injuries here were just as horrific as previous places we had visited on the way down the coast. A major goal was to stop infection so the supply of antiseptic went pretty quickly. We had kids who had been bitten by starving or frightened dogs, and babies with roaring temperatures caused by we didn't know what. We were not doctors, but we had to act like we were. And people would often come up to us without having anything really wrong with them – they just wanted us to touch them and let them know that things would be alright. After some of them had been treated they would get down on the ground and kiss our feet, so appreciative were they.

After several hours of providing first-aid it was decided that the school library should be cleaned out and used for accommodation and a field hospital. All that remained was the library and one two-storey classroom building. The high water mark could be seen a few tiles above the bottom of the library's roof line – I'd guess about four metres high. Debris from the school and other buildings had been washed inside, joining toppled school desks and the children's schoolwork, while papers and books were trapped in the grilles of the high vents. Crikey, if it had been a school day when the tsunami hit … well, I can't begin to imagine. I took some bizarre relief in the knowledge that this disaster could have been so much worse, if that was at all possible.

Once we cleared out the rubble inside the library, as many homeless people as could fit would sleep in it and in the remaining school building. They had no water, so their mouths were dry and children and adults gulped down the smallest amount from our bottles and licked their lips like they'd had the best champagne. So much good emanated from that library over the ensuing months, as thousands of people saw it as the base of our operations.

Somehow we had to get the people working, during the day at least, to make them constructive in rebuilding their village and to divert them from their grief. Night-time was such a different story. I remember the sobs of the mothers and fathers and kids … it sounded like the whole village was crying sometimes. It was heartbreaking and depressing; something that I'd never had to deal with before. I just had to leave the village at the end of the day; it was completely overwhelming, people throwing themselves about in fits, flailing arms and legs thrashing madly about.

The only person other than Chinthu who could speak good English was a woman called Chamilla and those two soon became our 'disciples', if you like. There was nowhere for us to stay in Peraliya so we headed to a little tourist town called Hikkaduwa, four kilometres further down the road towards Galle. We came upon the Casa Lanka guesthouse which had thirteen rooms costing $5 a night. It was closer to backpacker accommodation than a luxury resort – rooms had fans but no air-conditioning and there was no swimming pool, just an open-air bar and restaurant. In our eyes, though, it was a five-star retreat compared to the place we'd just left.

Hikkaduwa, which was not as badly smashed by the tsunami as Peraliya because it was protected by the reef, was initially a fishing village, like Peraliya, but in the 1960s it started promoting tourism, and its surf is quite famous and popular for surfboard riders from all over the world. I think there are probably a dozen hotels and guesthouses there, the biggest one being the 156-room Coral Gardens Hotel, but you could hardly call it a resort town. It was a beautiful setting, though, overlooking the ocean with lovely white sand and palm trees. Casa Lanka had been knocked around by the tsunami a bit but upstairs was fairly unscathed. The family that owned the guesthouse was really grateful for having us there, because our payment helped them get back on their feet as well; tourists were rare for quite some time after the tsunami.

I roomed at first with our driver, Toyna, and found him to be a level-headed, down-to-earth devoted Muslim. In those first few weeks he taught me to be more humble, less cantankerous and more patient. He and Bruce were the soothing influences on me of an evening as we de-stressed – always reiterating messages like 'have faith, things will work out', 'don't rush', 'little by little' and 'don't lose hope, the people need you' as I went about my business like a bull at a gate.

It was at Casa Lanka of an evening, when we would finally ease down and have a meal and a few drinks, where I got to know better my other three colleagues – Bruce French, Alison Thompson and Oscar Gubernati. The verandah and downstairs 'beer garden' area became our debriefing 'surgery' of a night where we would let go of all our feelings and describe our day. Someone amongst us would pick up the camera and record our confessionals and these were later turned into an integral part of *The Third Wave* documentary.

Bruce, Alison and Oscar were all very different people, drawn together by the same compassionate view on life.

Bruce was certainly an interesting character. He lived in a yurt in the mountains outside of Telluride, a ski resort town in the Rocky Mountains in Colorado 3000 metres high in the San Juan Range. He usually worked six months a year for touring bands as they travelled around the world; he had served meals to not only the Red Hot Chilli Peppers and Pearl Jam but also to Neil Young, the Grateful Dead, Rush and a few others. He specialised in meals for people with special dietary demands and had worked on luxury yachts too, as well as for people in his home town. He loved surfing as well as skiing and was just one of those laidback guys – I described him as being 'zen' – who had a massive heart of gold and a clear head, a guy who just loved making mankind feel at peace. Bruce had stopped off in Galle in the early 1990s when he was on the crew of a boat in an around-the-world sailboat race, and during his three-week stopover he rented an old motorbike, which broke down too many times but which also gave him an opportunity to immerse himself in Sinhalese culture. When he saw what had happened in the tsunami, he knew Sri Lanka had the fewest resources to cope with a disaster of such magnitude, and hopped on a plane to help.

Alison, from southern Sydney in Australia, was the daughter of a church minister father and a mother who was a nurse, so she had an interesting upbringing which included spending some time in Third World countries with her parents on their missionary trips. She had wanted to play women's cricket for Australia and was apparently pretty good at it, but she had a car accident shortly before the Aussie team was to be picked one year and she couldn't walk properly for a couple of years. She became a mathematics teacher but loved travelling and had seen plenty of the world, including Antarctica. She moved to New York when she was in her late twenties, worked on Wall Street for a while and attended film school at New York University. After she saw reports of the devastation from the attack on the Twin Towers on 11 September 2001, Alison rollerbladed down to the World Trade Center and decided to volunteer to help administer first-aid. She spent nine months volunteering in her spare time at Ground Zero. She was very compassionate, a real busy-beaver personality who threw herself right into whatever she focused on, and I got the feeling she experienced a lot more emotion than she showed, but felt she had to keep things inside so she could keep going and never lose sight of the big picture; plus she reckoned she had an Italian boyfriend whose Sicilian temper at times ensured he was abusive and emotional enough for the both of them (Alison's words not mine, Oscar, buddy)!

Oscar was a high-spirited Italian who had grown up in Palermo, the capital of Sicily. He moved to Los Angeles in 1990 to undertake film studies at UCLA and went into a production company based at Universal Studios where he started producing independent films. He moved to New York in 2002 to establish a production company called Ozone Pictures, and it was through the film industry that he met Alison. While Oscar and Alison were passionate about the film industry, I do believe their major motive for going to Sri Lanka was to do what they could to make a difference in the clean-up, and that was obvious in the endless exhausting hours they spent helping others. Filming their efforts allowed them to take the incredible story to the big screen to motivate others to help people in need. Oscar was the business mind, the manager figure, during our time in Peraliya. We butted heads a few times because we were the strongest willed and most outspoken of the four of us. We didn't hold back our feelings, but I love him like I do Alison and Bruce, as you would anyone you spent so much time with in such circumstances. As a foursome, we just gelled, proving that opposites can work in a group, complementing and inspiring each other, especially when we had such a strong shared motivation driving us.

After our first night at our new home in Hikkaduwa, Toyna took us back to Peraliya. He was our private chauffeur for the first few weeks before we moved into separate hotels and hired tuk-tuks to go back to Peraliya each morning; they virtually became our private taxi drivers and our regular business helped feed a few more families. On our second day in Peraliya there were still blank faces although a few smiles were starting to come forth, especially from the children. It became very much about us winning the hearts and minds and assuring the people that we were there to help them and they shouldn't be afraid of us. I think our energy rubbed off on them.

I picked up bricks from the ground and started to clean up a little bit, and then other people started to follow. I think they thought, 'Well, if this white man, a stranger, can do it, I can too.' They just needed some firm guidance. A lot of the volunteers who filtered through Peraliya in the coming weeks would say, 'Geez, you're a bit hard on these people at times, Donny. You're pretty noisy and boisterous.' Well I think, quite frankly, that's what they needed. They needed my energy to sort of get them out of that place they were in, really; they needed a stern but caring voice. I'd like to think my 'no nonsense' type of leadership I'd learned in the army came in handy in motivating people.

It must have been so demoralising for them to see the occasional supply truck or earth-moving equipment and the like drive past their village while they sat there as the forgotten tribe of Sri Lanka. And those that did detour were mostly there just to worship the train or take photos. Not that there were many trucks because, for all the efforts of the NGOs (non-government organisations) that were getting worldwide credit from the media, and all the government-backed aid that was supposed to have been dispersed, very little saw any part of the 100 kilometres or so of coast between Colombo and Galle for quite a few months. When the NGOs did come our way, I believe that some just wanted to fly the biggest flag in front of the biggest area and were, in some ways, competing against each other as opposed to helping each other – not that I am bagging the motives of NGOs, because some in particular were to be godsends for Peraliya.

The four of us soon took on 'special task' assignments and unofficial titles. Alison was in charge of first-aid and she made a bandana with a red cross on it, out of a scarf, I think, so she could be easily identified as a 'nurse' – although she revealed later it was also to shield her from the lice on many of the unfortunate people she treated. Oscar became the main negotiator and coordinated the allocation of funds and the volunteer help that began to flood into the village within the next few weeks. Bruce took care of logistics, like the storage of food and other supplies, and the cooking, and had almost a full-time job keeping me sane! I became head of construction, if you like, arranging for temporary and permanent housing and getting sanitary and water services built. To look the part, the chief gave me an orange workman's vest, like you see roadside workers or construction signalmen wear. We sort of became a modern-day Village People, as far as looks went anyway.

We decided on day two that we had to clean out the temple so that the people could pray; that was obviously integral to their healing process, so that became a primary task for the next couple of days. But the main thing was to somehow feed the people so there wouldn't be more deaths. To this end, one day early on Oscar and I stopped a truck which was on the way to Galle and acted like aid officers, instructing it to unload its wares. It seemed too easy; I'd stand there with my orange vest, walkie-talkie and big stick which made me look 'official' to a degree, and Oscar spoke to them and indicated where they should go and unload. Sometime in that first week he also commandeered an earth-mover bound for somewhere else. When you think of it, we could have been jailed and charged for obstructing aid services or something, but the people of Peraliya were desperate for food and we had to find some way of delivering it. Then I met this lovely gentleman from a town inland and told him what a problem lack of water was. He came back the next day with a truckload of fresh bottled water.

We had to build a trench of some sort for people to crap in; sanitation was a big problem. By day two we had acquired some shovels and I assigned Luke and Steve (the two pilots who we met on the way down from Colombo and who'd stayed to help) to co-opt a few local men to dig a slit-trench about 3 metres by 1.5 metres deep. It wasn't rocket science, just a hole in the ground bordered by a screen of shade cloth the two of them had picked up along the way, but it was a big breakthrough just the same. It was Peraliya's first post-tsunami public toilet! That first building project also occupied some of the men who otherwise could find nothing to do. I thought, 'If we can keep these people busy during the day, it will take their minds off this terrible, terrible stuff that's happened to them.' So from that second day, for eight to ten hours a day, we'd try to keep them as busy as possible and for the other fourteen to sixteen hours they could grieve or whatever they wanted.

The children posed a different challenge. Many had lost their parents and had been taken under the wing of relatives or friends. Some had no one to care for them, so they stayed together in a group. The children no longer had the daily routine of going to school because the school was out of action and most of the teachers had died. They had no toys, not much shelter in the stinking heat which reached thirty-five degrees Celsius just about every day, and they were too scared to go swimming in the ocean. So we'd play with the kids when we had a chance, and chase them; anything to maybe put a smile on their faces for just a few moments. The smiles of the children produced the energy that kept us going, and if it wasn't for those children, we might have walked away a few weeks later as jealousy, inter-village rivalry and the feeling of desperation sank in to many people who realised they had nothing.

In those first few days we forged some trusting relationships with a core of people who became our deputies. We certainly had to get the chief onside, so as basic timber and nails and tools came in, I made sure his was the first temporary shelter we built. We never made any major decision without his approval; that's how the culture of those small villages worked. We'd have a meeting every morning with the chief and the elders and decide a schedule of activity. Oscar would always say if he called a meeting for 7.30 am we might start by 9.30; the concept of time is not something the Sri Lankans have much regard for, as we learned. We had to have some sort of list of priority tasks, and high on it was the building of temporary homes – there were only about ten families out of 550 whose houses were left standing.

It's weird that it took a few days for it to completely hit home to me that it was *the* train I had seen on the TV news bulletins standing there as a constant backdrop to the village, and that it was where more than 1600 people had met their deaths, plus over 250 from the village, many of whom we uncovered scattered under rubble and inland over the next three months. It hit me like a ton of bricks one day when I was looking at it and it became more than an abandoned train but evidence of just how many lives were lost in Peraliya. As I've said, when there was this endless parade of people stopping off to examine it, we thought, 'Stuff it, we're not going to let them come here and turn a blind eye to the devastation of the people who survived,' so we organised for the children to have collection buckets for donations. We had them line up to form a 'guard of honour', and we collected a reasonable amount of money which went into purchasing food and building materials.

When Steve and Luke left we were down to four people with a mountainous task that intimidated us, but we had become so dedicated to helping these people there was no way we were going to walk away. Bit by bit, brick by brick, was all we could do to help. My days would start at 5.30 am and often I wouldn't get back to Casa Lanka until eight or nine at night. Day by day the people of Peraliya gained trust in us. I'd walk around the village early every morning and say 'G'day' to nearly everybody – it was important for them to know that we were still there and hadn't abandoned them, that somebody cared about them.

About a week after we arrived we had a visit from the Sri Lankan Minister for Trade and Commerce, Mr Jeyaraj Fernandopulle, who stated that this part of the country was indisputably the worst affected, far more so than the eastern provinces he had just come from on a tour of inspection. He became a great ally from that day on, and he delivered on his promise to get us some army staff, and even police, who were stationed at the edge of the village to help us keep things in order. We had bulldozers and engineers and building materials which made the restoration of the village so much easier to achieve. In him we had a high-ranking government official we could call when we needed some resources. He seemed a very sympathetic man and it was clear he was seen as a pretty important dude by the villagers, so it gave them new hope when he walked around the place. He was very inquisitive about why I, and the others, had come to Peraliya and I didn't know how to explain it other than saying it was 'some sort of calling'.

It was quite bizarre, though understandable when you think about it, but the people of the village thought we belonged to one of the big aid organisations; that we were part of an organised group assigned to help them. After seeing us talking at length with Mr Fernandopulle and also signalling trucks full of supplies to a halt, that was probably logical. It was about three weeks into our stay, when four or five other volunteers who had heard about our plight joined our little project, and Bruce said to me: 'Donny, these people don't realise that we aren't from, you know, a proper organised relief group.' We'd never pretended we were anything but a small group of individuals, so in a way it was a compliment that they thought we were organised, experienced aid workers.

That had its positive and negative sides. The positive was that we could make our own decisions and not be held back by red tape and approval systems; the negative was that the villagers thought we had access to the millions of dollars of funding and all the labour services that they had heard about. It took a lot of convincing them that that wasn't the case and some people would never be convinced that we didn't have a bottomless pit of money, especially after we distributed what private contributions we received to some individual families (more of that later). We were just four people who had little money and relied on donations from friends and contacts in our home countries and from those passing by. We put up a sign that said 'Relief Camp Peralya' which looked far from professional, especially when it was spelt incorrectly (the 'i' was hastily added). It acted as a magnet for people travelling on the Galle Road to stop and have a look at our 'project', and it attracted some donations and volunteer labour. It was ironical, too, that while the villagers of Peraliya were angry at the government and the largest aid organisations, believing they had turned their backs on them and not directed any of the perceived pot of gold their way, other villages along the coastline were jealous that so much was done at Peraliya, and thought that it must have received favoured treatment from officials. That just wasn't the case.

Peraliya was struggling to come to grips with the tsunami's devastation, like any village along the coast. The thing I found toughest to come to grips with personally, was the dead remains. I had to brace myself when I came across bodies in the rubble and I had to adopt the mindset that there was nothing I could do for them, other than maybe take them to where they might be identified and have a proper burial. But confronting dead bodies brought the two fatal car crashes in Perth back to my mind, especially at night when I tried to sleep. Then two incidents happened while I was in Sri Lanka that added to my mental misery and were the toughest experiences to take. As much as I would like to forget both, I can't shake them from my memory.

Once a week, after the children had become comfortable getting back into the ocean (and that took some doing), we would take them to Hikkaduwa for a swim and to buy them ice cream;

well, mostly Alison and Oscar and some helpers would. Other times we'd make sure we took some time out to play with them or take them for a walk along the beach; it was as much a relief for us from the exhausting work in the unbearable heat as it was a treat for the kids. But one of those walks turned into a nightmare. It's in the film. I don't know who was with me carrying the camera, I think Toyna. Anyway, we came across a body washed up on the beach. When I stopped, I realised it was a boy and he had no head, his arms had been cut off at the shoulders and his legs had been severed below the knees. And he was still attached to a wooden stake by rope. That didn't happen in the tsunami.

One of the children said, 'Let's pick it up by the legs,' before we stepped in to take them away from the body as soon as possible. Unusually, there was no odour whatsoever coming from the corpse. We quickly buried the body before someone else came across it. I was very traumatised; I still get flashbacks. Had that poor body been tortured? Who knows with the ongoing troubles between the Tamils and Sinhalese, and even the brutality of the inter-village gang rivalry we later learned about. How could a young boy be so cruelly mutilated? Sadly, it wasn't the only body I saw washed up on the shore; there were plenty of others, and some had something missing from their torsos – a hand or an arm or something. I never got used to it; I just learned to deal with it. I know it sounds harsh but there was nothing I could do for them, so in a way, that was a closed book. It was the people who died well after the tsunami hit, people I knew and became so fond of, that caused me more grief.

The incident that affected me even more was when a young man in a tuk-tuk was hit by one of the crazy trucks that used to race each other from town to town. It happened probably fifty metres from a hospital on the outskirts of Galle. You would think someone from the hospital would have come out to help, but no – no one lifted a finger except for Seb (that's Dr Sebastian Pluese from Germany) and me. I was screaming for help and for someone to get this or that but nobody could speak English, so nobody understood what I was saying. We gave the guy CPR and I opened his mouth to get some air into his lungs but his jaw was just all split and his teeth were hanging out. I thought, 'Fuck, man, there's no way I can give him a breath of air.' Seb told me to use my hands to make a funnel and just sort of blow that way, but there was nothing we could do for this poor guy.

Finally someone came from the hospital and put him on a trolley and wheeled him into their version of the emergency department, but still no one seemed interested in helping, even when we shouted to them to come to our assistance. We learned later that apparently medical people in Sri Lanka are reluctant to help accident victims (and there would be hundreds of them every day) for fear of legal action against them if treatment is not successful; I don't know if that is true or not. Finally we got someone to put the defibrillator on him – it was the first time I'd ever seen the 'paddles' used – but he was too far gone by then. He died in a pool of blood in front of us.

The terrible pity of it, I later learned, was that he'd just picked up a new tuk-tuk and had been riding down to the hardware store to get some timber to build himself a little shelter for it off the side of his house. Sebastian and I went to the family, spoke to his mother and ended up giving her 20,000 rupees so they could have a proper burial. There might have been a little bit left over to help the family through, as the dead man had been the main breadwinner.

That haunted me for a long time – the third young person in my life dying in front of me in a motor accident. But as soon as I got back to Peraliya I sought some counselling from an Israeli psychologist who had been working in the village with the Israeli aid team, and that helped me enormously, but it still affects me today – how could it not? That sad episode, however, bonded Sebastian and me even more closely together. He said to me one night that I was the best unqualified 'paramedic' that he had seen, which was a wonderful thing to say and boosted my confidence no end.

Back in Peraliya, the more rubble we cleaned up, the more bodies we kept coming across. We didn't see many at first but once the army engineers came in and we had bulldozers at work, we came across a lot more. We were still discovering bodies well into April, except by then they weren't bodies, they were just bones. We would try to find somebody who might recognise them by a piece of jewellery or clothing. My able lieutenant Kumara had lost his wife, his two daughters and his sister, and every time someone found a body, whether it was around Peraliya or inland, he would be the first one there to see if it was one of his. It was heart-wrenching to see this young man, who I dealt with every day, so dejected when a body wasn't one of his family's. He just wanted to find some remnant of them, or to know where they were found. He never did, and that saddens me so much.

There was no morgue, and I didn't want to know too much about what happened to the bodies before they were buried; Alison took care of that. Sometimes she would put limbs in ladies' handbags or garbage bags because we couldn't keep up the supply of body bags. People would walk up to her sometimes with an arm or hand or other body part and give them to her like they were children's toys that needed putting away. She said at the time: 'I try not to think about the bodies; sometimes I pretend I am at the butcher's and am picking up meat. It helps me with the reality of what I am really holding in my hands. Whatever it takes to get through this, right? The bodies I find are unrecognisable and full of flies and maggots.' Some bodies had the hands chopped off them by thieves wanting their jewellery; other times body parts had been chewed by famished dogs. It is something that still disturbs me and I never, ever got used to seeing or even hearing about it. It was fucking horrid.

The mass grave we had there was once exhumed by an organisation – Interpol, I think – in an effort to find the remains of a couple of foreigners, which they did. Even when we only found a few limbs, if they could be identified we still put them in coffins and they had a proper burial. It was horrific at times; you'd be working somewhere and then all of a sudden you'd find somebody's hip, their femur, tibia or fibula, or a foot. You wouldn't smell it until it was on the surface; it was like cracking an egg open, a rotten egg – phew, it just hit you.

Dogs started to bring body parts back to the village from wet areas a few kilometres away and the risk of disease was a great concern, especially as the dogs would be licking the children, and quite a few dogs began getting sick. So we had to order body bags from wherever we could get them – the Sri Lankan government for starters – and go and bag as many corpses as we could find lying in shallow water or buried in mud as the water level subsided.

About a month into our stay there were days when we had to get an expedition together and go inland to recover bodies. Alison had become known as the 'Body Collector' by then – somehow she had steeled herself for the almost daily occurrence of being presented with part of, or all of, a dead person.

Sometimes we would recover twenty bodies or body parts a day. We would never let her go out searching for corpses without one of us – Bruce, Oscar or myself – with her. This was hard work, physically and emotionally, but we had to deal with it and think, 'The least I can do for these people is to give them a decent burial and maybe give their relatives some closure if they can identify them.' I'd often wear a face mask when on body collecting duties; I just couldn't stand that smell of death. I remember one lady was identified by the dress she was wearing; it was recovered only 150 metres from the remains of her house and her son insisted she be buried on the house block. It seemed there was a constant flow of funerals for months.

Quite a few people committed suicide while I was there. One man I got to know well hanged himself. And I can't judge them – how would you recover from your spouse and children being taken from you? Then there was a man in the village with no legs who starved to death, like he just lost his will to live. We made a special trip to Colombo to get him a wheelchair but, after seeing what happened to his family and friends in the tsunami and not being able to help at all because of his handicap, he just withered away. That was tough to take. There were others who died in different circumstances, too, but I don't want to release the memories anymore than I have to here; many cases I have locked away.

The thing that drove us to keep going the most, no matter how tough it got, were the children. So many had lost their parents, or their entire family, and some had wandered in from other villages and towns when word got around that we had food and medical supplies, and they would attach themselves to the main group of kids and stay. In the end we sent them to an orphanage that we helped rebuild in Galle.

Someone must have donated a heap of clothes early in the piece because the kids always seemed to have nice new clothes on. But in the first week or two, it didn't hide their gloomy personalities. They'd lost their family members, their homes, their possessions, their school, their love of the ocean, because of what it had so cruelly done to them and their daily routine. Plus the village leaders, who would normally have assured them that everything would be okay in their lives, had become so traumatised and demotivated by what had happened, the children had lost that security as well.

Alison suggested we get the kids to draw and act out their feelings on paper; for the first few weeks all they drew were large waves and bodies, people standing on houses, bodies floating in water, some without heads, and crumbled buildings. Then after a while they started to draw pictures of us and the new houses we'd built. That showed how their thoughts had changed, that they had progressed in dealing with the trauma of the tsunami, and that the healing was under way. They'd identify me by my slouch hat, stick and orange vest and Alison by the red cross. The children are definitely what kept us going when we were exhausted and often frustrated by the demands of the adults, who seemed to want more the more we did for them.

I think it was Oscar and a journalist from Britain, James, who came up with the idea of a system of photo identification tags for the children. There were reports of child kidnappings along the coast. I never came across any direct evidence of that, but other people certainly heard first-hand what was supposedly going on. Alison learned of two French nurses who saw a girl being taken away from an orphanage by two people who showed fake papers to suggest they had government approval to 'adopt' the girl, or maybe that they were her parents. They were allowed to take her away screaming. I'm sure a lot of the places hit by the tsunami, where so many kids were left homeless and orphaned, became prime targets for pedophiles. James and his friend Paola worked hard to ensure all the children in the village had ID tags hanging around their necks to protect them, and we thought the aid workers may as well have them, too, so people knew who we were.

You couldn't help but be inspired and uplifted by the pure innocence and energy of the children and the fact that they –

once they learned to again – would smile, and laugh, and play, and follow you and want to touch you and make you feel special – when they had absolutely nothing left in the wake of the tsunami.

We needed them. After a few weeks you could see the physical change in us. We all looked so drawn and exhausted. I would get to work before the sun came up and work until after dark and would only have fruit for breakfast, some rice and dhal most days (sometimes we wouldn't eat during the day) and then a basic rice meal of a night to give us sustenance, although Bruce could make most things taste good. We couldn't keep enough water in our bodies because it was very hot all the time. I developed 'drop foot' – a condition where you turn your foot inwards and toes downwards when walking, so rather than heel-toe, heel-toe, it is toe-heel, toe-heel – and had a lower back problem and bad knees, so I was walking along and often falling over. But there was no way any of us was quitting. Help, at times from the most unexpected sources, was soon on the way. Peraliya became a mecca for so many kind-hearted people from all walks of life who, like us, wanted to make a difference to these unfortunate Sri Lankans, no matter how small that was. It was bloody amazing when you think of it: the place the world had forgotten became a magnet for people from all over the world.

6

WE ARE NOT ALONE

For the first two weeks in Peraliya we didn't see one NGO, government or aid organisation grant of money and we were piecing together the village and its residents' lives on handouts. But, like a gift from heaven, suddenly we were not alone. Aid groups started coming and providing people and materials. Peraliya, it seemed, was on the map of disaster hotspots. You little ripper! A major reason was that Alison, through the help of some friends back in New York, I think, created a website (you can still go to it: www.peraliya.com) and started recording a daily diary, initially from an internet café in Hikkaduwa and eventually from a computer at Casa Lanka. She appealed for help in Peraliya, pushing it as a place where people didn't have to have specialist skills or go through the screening process that the NGOs insisted on before you could join them as aid-workers. As she said on the website: *Volunteers Just Come!! Everyone is welcome: no skills required!!!! See you here!!*

Bugger me, the advertising worked. By week three of our 'project' we had six or so more volunteers and a steady stream of people then came through Peraliya over the next four months; some stayed on longer than I did! Other than the website, there was strong word of mouth between people who knew, or knew of, someone who had passed through, and the little village sort of became famous as a place where there was no red tape, no strict approval process, no judgment of character, no need for any particular skill – just a human bank of souls with a compassionate heart and a willingness to dig in and give it a go. Of course the fact that it was the site of the world's worst ever train disaster also drew people to it.

People then started wandering into the village, both individual helpers like us and organised aid-workers, and they'd ask, 'Who's in charge?' Volunteers would point to the library or directly to Bruce, Alison, Oscar or me if we were in sight and say, 'They're in charge.' We weren't in charge, really; everything we did was with the approval of the chief and his village leaders. It was funny that highly trained, organised teams would come in and we'd give them directions, when in comparison we were the unskilled labour. But most people identified us as the project managers. The officers in charge would say, 'What do you want my men to do through the day?' – it was like I was the commanding officer. If only my old army buddies could have seen me.

We certainly didn't do everything right by the disaster handbook but we were in there having a go and we were able to succeed because we were not caught up in all the bullshit red tape, bureaucracy and the political crap others probably had to deal with. If we needed to dig a hole, we dug a hole. If we needed to give somebody Panadol, we gave them Panadol. We used common sense and the need for assistance as our guide book. Scottish medicos Dr Shouren and his wife taught me how to suture wounds. Their motto was 'see one, do one, show one' – in other words, see it done, do it yourself, then show someone else how to do it. So there we were, acting as doctors and closing up bad wounds. It's just like sewing up a bag of spuds.

Very early on, bottles of Coca-Cola arrived by the hundreds (directly from the local Coke distributors, I'd imagine) which was not just a real treat (for the kids particularly), but was good in settling some upset stomachs – even though the drinks were never refrigerated. Then USAID funded a heap of Sri Lankan volunteers, and hundreds came to earn money removing rubble and working as building labourers, but that also gave us more mouths to feed – and more casualties to treat, too, as they never wore shoes or any protection for their hands, so there were plenty of cuts and bruises. What we didn't take into account was all the domestic animals – mostly dogs and cats – that were starving, too, and were forced to go into contaminated areas to search for food, which, as I've said, increased the chance of disease spreading. Alison sort of adopted a couple of cats only for one of them to be stolen and presumably cooked and eaten by some starving family. That shows how desperate people were.

When Mr Fernandopulle got some army staff to lend us a hand with the removal of rubble and building of temporary shelters, and young Sri Lankan army engineers came and helped with construction and clearing, they were extremely valuable because they had equipment like chainsaws – not the most efficient ones, but at least ones that worked. They were great guys, highly motivated, and their commanding officer was a tremendous person; we built up a very good working rapport and he would often ask me for input. Mr Fernandopulle certainly showed his devotion to Peraliya by sending in teams and resources within days of his visit. To be honest, I loved working with them and it was interesting to see how another country's army operated. We even had US Marines come to help for a few days but, for some bureaucratic reason, they were not allowed to enter the village. So we pushed the rubble to the other side of the road where they were able to pick it up and truck it away, which was a massive help.

A senior German paramedic, Reinhold Klosterman from Hamelyn, came through one day on a reconnaissance visit to see which were the worst affected areas and how resources could best be allocated. He flew back to Germany and said he would return in a week with a full set of paramedics; we didn't know whether it was wishful thinking or not but, bugger me, not only did he bring half a dozen others, he brought a heap of medical supplies as well – real cutting-edge stuff. They were just amazing, those guys, dead-set lifesavers, literally. Suddenly we didn't have to stretch well beyond our medical capabilities in treating some of the more serious injuries. The medical supplies enabled us to have a genuinely well-equipped medical centre with fridges. Even a tablecloth was a big thing to have, as was shade cloth on the windows to cool the room down. These improvements, though, brought even more people from other towns or villages that didn't have access to any basic medical service. Some would spend just about all the money they had to hire a tuk-tuk to take them to Peraliya for treatment then take them back home again. Some women walked ten kilometres to get treatment, that's how desperate they were.

The extra resources freed me up from assisting Alison with the first-aid to concentrate on other important things, such as the tasks I referred to as the three Rs – 'Reclaim, Recycle and Rebuild'. We connected water and electricity to newly built houses, mostly using

Sri Lankan plumbers, electricians and tilers. We'd always try to organise labour from within the village if possible, but if not, from outside. Dinesh, who I often talk about, was an electrician from another village, Dodanduwa; he was the only Sri Lankan tradesman who came to Peraliya and asked what he could do without expecting to receive any payment. He got a lot of work from me, and I insisted I paid him but never at overinflated prices; he still had to do the job at the right price. I felt good that he and his family were well looked after because of his initiative and work ethic. Dodanduwa lost quite a few boats but did not have many damaged buildings; we managed to send some workers to help build huts so the the fishermen could repair their boats and nets under cover.

The Danish People's Aid (DPA), which is a completely volunteer-run organisation from Denmark, was absolutely fantastic in sending over first-aid supplies, plus workers and food. The DPA provided building supplies for over 700 temporary shelters in and around Peraliya. It also had lots of women counsellors to help out with the Sri Lankan women. There were German, Austrian and Danish water experts who were able to get large water tanks in and connect them up to homes and other buildings, and repair the wells that had been destroyed or contaminated during the tsunami. The German organisation Technisches Hilfswerk (THW), a specialist natural disaster relief program, was fantastic, in that regard.

The Israeli aid team force brought about ten trauma therapists and psychologists into the village and they were a massive help. They started counselling those who had lost family members and took over entertaining and occupying the kids each day. They had them singing and laughing, and you can see them in a poignant scene in the documentary where, with Oscar helping them, they are doing crazy mime and dance movements. Oscar was certainly wonderful with the kids. The children were regularly laughing and by now had a lot more life in them, and that lifted the spirits of all the volunteers and the residents.

As I've said, it was very hard to get the children to go back into the water, though, because they were so afraid of it after the tsunami. Little by little we coaxed them in a bit deeper, taking a group down and linking arms so they knew they would be safe. At first some pointed to the horizon and screamed out, 'Big wave,' and ran back to the sand. Eventually they would go down by themselves and run around and splash, and the Israelis were wonderful in monitoring this and encouraging the kids.

We had a Texan minister, a fantastic guy called Larry Buck from Bread for a Hungry World, and he provided money for replacement boats and other goods. He also gave us 'original four' a personal donation to help us fund our accommodation and food, which was so welcome as we had little money and were relying on funds being sent to us from home. I got a job with the

Danish People's Aid as the temporary shelter construction supervisor, getting 1500 rupees a day (about A$19), which was enough to pay for food, washing and refreshments. I was able to afford to go 'upmarket' with my accommodation to an air-conditioned room in a hotel that had a pool and provided beautiful tropical fruit for breakfast. Between Larry and the DPA, that was the only funding I received outside of help from home, and it was enough to keep me going with my little luxuries.

Even Australian cricketer Shane Warne and the other great spinner in world cricket, Muttiah Muralitharan, dropped in for a couple of hours on a goodwill tour along the Colombo–Galle coast in early February. I met them and had a bit of a chat and they were great, playing with the children and lifting the spirits of the locals. Muralitharan comes from the city of Kandy and is one of the few Tamils to have played Test cricket for Sri Lanka, while Warney rated the cricket ground at Galle, where he'd played Tests against Sri Lanka, as one of his favourite grounds in the world – no doubt because he took his 500th Test wicket there the previous March (a few wickets ahead of 'Murali'). The Galle ground was completely wiped out in the tsunami and Test cricket wasn't played there again until December 2007. Word got around quickly among the volunteers that Warne's charity organisation, the Shane Warne Foundation, donated a large sum of money towards the relief efforts; I heard $1 million, although that was never confirmed. Oh, and English cricket legend Ian Botham dropped into Peraliya too during a tour of tsunami-affected areas.

The kind-heartedness wasn't restricted to people who came from overseas. It might have seemed a small thing to others but I was overwhelmed one day when I had to make a rushed trip to a dentist at Ambalangoda to treat a really bad toothache. He drilled and filled the tooth and I was over the moon with relief from the pain. I asked how much I owed him and he wouldn't let me pay; he said in his broken English something like: 'You come to help my people, the least I can do is help you in your hour of need.' Just that little gesture meant something to me. While on that subject, a team of dentists came to the coastal strip but they were only equipped to remove teeth, not having brought any amalgam to fill them. They knew that fillings could not be maintained after they left so it was an attitude of 'lift them or leave them'.

I also had my local 'deputies' who worked as tirelessly as any of the overseas volunteers or army personnel assigned to help us. Chinthu became my right-hand man and Dinesh became my left-hand man, with Kumara remaining a very able ally. Then there was Chamilla, the woman translator and one of the few Christians in the village – well, maybe the only one, I think, in a Buddhist region. She was a very kind-hearted woman. She told Alison she had prayed every night for God to send someone to help, and that 'someone' was us. She became an integral part of our team as well, a lovely woman, but ultimately she paid the price for her association with us when some turned against her, believing she was getting handouts the other villagers weren't, although that certainly wasn't the case. For months Chamilla, her husband and her daughter lived in the library turned medical centre, along with others, and didn't complain that many families were given shelters before she was. She and her husband kept it immaculately clean, while she was on call virtually 24/7 if we needed a translator. Mostly she was used at the medical centre itself so that the many Sri Lankans who came for treatment could communicate what was wrong with them.

Chinthu, who I had a great rapport with from day one because of our army connection, was given extended leave from the Sri Lankan services to help his village. He was a very confident young man of twenty who was well respected in the village and proved to be very loyal to us; he was someone you could assign a task to and he would handle it and follow it through well. He was lucky that he'd lost none of his family members in the tsunami, so he didn't have to bear the grief that Kumara did, for example. Chinthu used to love trying to copy my Aussie accent, and sayings like 'that's the go' became second nature to him as an expression of encouragement. His accent was crap though (sorry, buddy).

Kumara, a sniper in the army and a very fit and athletic young man, was a more complex person who was badly haunted by what happened in the tsunami. He was out at sea fishing when it hit, so far out it was nothing but a largish wave that went past his boat. When he got to shore he quickly realised the devastation that had been dealt his people – and that his wife, two daughters and a sister had perished. His father was an alcoholic and was of no comfort to him (I learned little about his mother). Kumara carried a lot of anger and grief, and while he was a hard worker and eager to please as we did our grinding work, he struggled emotionally every single day.

Dinesh was a wonderful young bloke, and while we paid him market rates for his services, he went well above and beyond the call of duty, as did Chinthu and Kumara. Dinesh was the softly spoken, unassuming one – the opposite of Kumara – but he always liked to find the humour in a situation or crack a joke to lighten the mood. He came from a beautiful family in which he was the major breadwinner, and he was just so committed to what he did. Dinesh taught me the wonderful joy of family and what really mattered in this life, and how to stay centred and in touch with everything around me.

Unfortunately he suffered a terrible trauma while we were there and we organised for him to have some counselling, so worried were we about its effect. What happened was this: we needed a 44-gallon drum to be cut in half so we could use it to burn rubbish and also as a grille for a barbecue, so I asked Dinesh if he knew someone who could do the job. He suggested a young friend of his who volunteered to prepare the drum in his village. Dinesh's friend took to the task with an oxy-torch, but unfortunately didn't realise you're supposed to fill a petrol drum with water first to neutralise the fumes. Once he hit it with the oxy-torch it blew up instantly and killed him. That really rocked Dinesh, who felt responsible; I did too because I was the one who had asked for the task to be completed and just assumed the kid had done it before and knew what he was doing. It was yet another tragic tale which still brings tears to my eyes all these years later.

Toyna, of course, was another one of our Sri Lankan inner circle, along with Sunil, who worked virtually full-time as the cameraman for Alison and Oscar, as they filmed hour upon hour of our work for their documentary. Toyna stayed in Peraliya with us for the first couple of months or so, although he went back to Colombo on a few occasions – once for Ramadan, I remember – but he sent a friend down to take over his duties. Toyna also went beyond his paid role to help us; the spirit of those people who were assigned as our helpers was just fantastic.

Peraliya became the place where volunteers could come and know that they would be welcomed and utilised, if not in Peraliya itself then in other villages like Seenigama and Telwatta up and down the coast. We also farmed people off to Galle where we renovated the orphanage, after a message had leaked through to us that it had become overburdened with tsunami orphans and help was needed restoring it.

Unfortunately, that led to an extraordinary drama that still leaves me a little traumatised. I went down there once or twice a week for close to two months to check on progress and help supervise after allocating some of our volunteers to restoration work. We were really proud of what we did there; Wal, a New Zealand carpenter, and Greg, an American volunteer, did some great work and we had murals painted on the walls and we repainted the place inside and out. We even used to send volunteers down there to lift the spirits of the kids and to entertain them. But one downside of people lobbing up in a Third World country and offering help is that there is no vetting of their bona fides and you tend to take people at face value. It wasn't until a few weeks after I'd returned home that I received an email telling me the guy running the orphanage for those couple of months, an American I had always found a bit of a wanker actually, was a convicted pedophile, drug runner and fraudster.

This guy was there with his girlfriend and was using an alias. Apparently he'd only been released from a Mexican jail a few months earlier after being convicted of drug offences. He conned his way into taking over the orphanage in Sri Lanka but he was only there two months before shooting through suddenly when the Sri Lankan Criminal Investigation Department wanted to question him after concerns were raised about his involvement and possible fraud. It sounds like he saw the tsunami as a way of making a quick buck. There were rumours that he took off with a fair amount of money that had been donated and he might have interfered with some children while there too; and there we were doing every thing we could to help him! Even the singer Sting donated money to the orphanage. I don't know whether the authorities ever caught up with him, but I doubt it. He may very well still be on the run somewhere.

We heard a lot of reports about corruption and people supposedly taking personal advantage of aid funds, so that cast suspicion over everyone – even all of the well-meaning of us in Peraliya. That was hard to cop at times but, hey, it was just part of the situation we were in – and I reckon a lot of foul business did go on.

One of the unpopular and controversial decisions made while we were in Sri Lanka was the government's directive that anyone who'd lost a home within 100 metres of the shoreline could not rebuild back on their plot, supposedly to ensure their safety if a tsunami or massive tide or major storm or flooding happened again. Many of these people were evacuated to Alluthawalla, about fifteen kilometres inland. Well over a thousand people were dumped into the jungle with nothing but a small pond to wash themselves in and tents that were provided as shelter. It must have been so heartbreaking for them; here were people whose lifeblood was fishing and they were miles inland without a fish or wave within cooee.

When we found out about their fate from some of the villagers, I thought I should make it a priority to help build some infrastructure, because after they were dumped there the government pretty well forgot them. The locals were very sceptical of the government's intentions; there were rumours going around that officials had disposed of the people within the 100-metre zone so the government could build resorts there in prime positions. I don't know if there was a speck of truth in it but time will certainly tell. The strange thing was why they evacuated and relocated those only within 100 metres of the ocean. The tsunami went way inland, and whether you were 100 metres or 500 metres away didn't make much difference. The tsunami had affected people three or four kilometres inland.

So I ended up spending a lot of time up there putting some sort of infrastructure in place to make it a little more habitable for the evacuees. I got some toilets built, and got a water bore dug for a well. We arranged to buy some pushbikes (and I think a few were donated) for some of them to be able to get back to Peraliya to see the ocean and friends. Alluthawalla was a picturesque setting if you were a tea, coffee or coconut farmer, but not if you were a fisherman. And these people were nothing but fishermen! They came from several coastal towns and villages and there were obvious inter-village rivalries and mistrust up there which caused some problems, as you would expect. They were getting food and water from aid organisations – I know the Israelis brought in cooking utensils and food. Some of the Sri Lankans brought livestock and seafood with them, and it would always be shared around as a communal thing. I guess they elected a chief of this newly created village, and some sort of hierarchical structure would have been put in place but, essentially, it was a refugee camp.

One of my best memories of Peraliya was the day the school reopened. It's another event captured brilliantly in *The Third Wave*. It was very emotional. First, Dibika, a woman from Hikkaduwa, who had been saving to go on an overseas holiday, used her money instead to provide white dresses and white shirts and blue shorts for all the children as school uniforms. She also raised money to get some books and shoes. What an amazing gesture; she was a special lady. The glow on the faces of the kids when they had these pristine-clean new uniforms made me cry; honestly, I was sobbing like a baby.

I was worse the day the school actually reopened. We had cleaned up the old desks with wire brushes, got them repaired and painted and put back into the school rooms. We painted the walls and put the blackboards back in place. We had a bit of a ceremony and I thought I was going to faint; my legs went rubbery and I just went into a corner and sobbed to myself. It was so nice to see the looks on the kids' faces and for them to get at least part of their school back; the lift it gave them to have their uniforms and classes back and a purpose and place to go to each day, a real sense of normality again, was just so obvious. It made me feel it was all worth it, that we had done something really good. I felt proud to be Australian, to be me. There must have been 150 to 200 children in the village. All of a sudden their eyes were wider and their smiles were bigger.

Then came the monsoons – the wet season – in February. We'd put a lot of temporary shelters where it previously hadn't flooded from rain but the tsunami had changed the terrain, and suddenly people were living up to their knees in water. On top of this a tide spilled over the Galle Road and the railway line into the village. All hands on deck, we tried to put in place temporary breakwaters to stop the flooding, but it was just band-aid treatment. Water gushed through many areas and just sat there. It was so demoralising, for us as well as the villagers. Diverting the water from these new low-lying spots, already water-logged from the monsoon, was just too hard. Till now, coping with monsoon floodwaters had been second nature to the locals, but with the lie of the land different because of the damage the tsunami had done, nothing was certain. People who had felt blessed to have a temporary shelter or the luxury of a new brick home suddenly had half a metre of water through their houses, so for a few days they had to go back to sleeping outside or in the temple, library or school.

We lost about four or five shelters out of the more than 400 we had built along the coastline, so that wasn't bad. However, we had a large mop-up job on our hands, which was made harder by the fact that the earth-moving equipment we'd previously been able to get from the army and other sources had gone; I think we got one backhoe. We sandbagged everywhere we could and hand-dug channels to take the water away from homes and the road, often in pouring rain. We couldn't even get a truck full of rubble to build some break-walls; it was just so hard with the resources we had, but we managed to stop a lot of the tide from getting to the most vulnerable parts of the village.

Disease was the biggest danger – cholera and dengue fever – especially for the children and the elderly. Dengue can spread even quicker than malaria and can have just as serious an effect, including death. That was another of our successes. I thought there would have been a much bigger problem with mosquitoes. At one stage I suggested getting a fogging machine full of insect spray to ward off the mozzies but we never needed that. It is amazing that we did not have any outbreak of disease the whole time we were there – again, the big fella upstairs must have been on our side.

We restored so much goodwill and peace to the village in those first few weeks, it was easy to overlook that this was a politically unstable part of the world. The population of Sri Lanka is mostly Buddhist Sinhalese while the largely Muslim Tamils are an Indian-origin ethnic group that spread into north-eastern Sri Lanka. Christians make up about eighteen per cent of the country's population. Since the 1980s the Tamils have been demanding their own independent state. When we were in Peraliya there had been a ceasefire since 2002 (this lasted until 2006) but naturally a lot of suspicion and unease still prevailed.

One day it was decided that, as we had more volunteers than we needed, we would send a group of people further down the coast where there had been little assistance offered, past Galle and then up to Batticaloa on the east coast, and I was assigned to go with the group on a three-day trip. Now, Batticaloa was regarded as a Tamil Tigers (the rebellion army) stronghold and it has a history of mysterious disappearances of strangers and mass murders and massacres. Nine of us went in two cars: Toyna and another young man drove our German doctor Sebastian, two Danish surfers (and builders) Jen and Jen (I assume it is the Danish version of John), Chinthu and two local monks, one from

Peraliya and one from Save the Children America, another organisation that helped us. Although we were told to be careful because it could be a pretty hairy place to go, we heard they desperately needed some aid just like everywhere else, so we took some medical supplies and toys for children.

Along the way we were bailed up at a roadblock by a couple of cadres, young Tamil women armed with AK47s. Shit, it was scary – they could have shot us and no one would have known what happened. Toyna was translating for us and we explained what we were there for, that Sebastian was a doctor and I was first-aid trained, and the monks had gifts for the children. They had their rifles pointing at us but once they realised we just wanted to help their people and they'd checked us out, the guns went down and all the tension went. We ended up treating some of their people and they were grateful just like anybody else at the end of the day.

The conflict between the Sinhalese and the Tamils was not our business. As far as we were concerned they were all Sri Lankans, and if they needed help, we would attempt to give it to them. We were not alone. Unbelievably, over 200 volunteers from twenty-three countries came to Peraliya and helped in some way during the five months of our 'project'– it really gives you faith in the human spirit. They came from Australia, the US, Italy, England, Ireland, Germany, France, Scotland, Denmark, Sri

Lanka, The Netherlands, Israel, Jamaica, Lichtenstein, New Zealand, the United Arab Emirates, South Africa, Austria, Singapore, Bavaria, Wales and Switzerland, and probably some other places, too, as I'm sure there were a few volunteers that didn't register. The library became a landmark, a beacon of hope. Sri Lankans knew if they came to Peraliya and that building, the white people would look after them.

As I said, it was exhausting, especially in heat and humidity that I'd never experienced before, and it was often emotional. But I felt good about myself for the first time in ten years. I felt good because of the way the kids looked, and because of the vibe I was getting off the locals who had taken me into their hearts and treated me as one of their own. I felt I had contributed to something that was far greater than anything I'd done in my life, or likely to do in my life. Naively, I threw the antidepressant tablets away shortly after the school reopened because I was feeling so strong in spirit. It was a stupid thing to do but I just felt so positive in my life and that I no longer had anything to be depressed about; I didn't need those dreaded things anymore.

My moods started to fluctuate within two days and I began to feel more anxious. People were telling me they noticed a difference in me, that I wasn't coping like I seemed to have been before. So I went back on the pills. Maybe the damage had been done, though, coming on top of physical exhaustion, the adaptation to a different diet, my crook knees getting sorer and weaker, and the mental exhaustion I was suffering. I hit the wall so powerfully and painfully, I thought I was going to die – that old Donny's number was up and the man upstairs had decided I had done my godly duties and it was time to join him.

7

MELTDOWN

I think it was 12 March. It had been around nine weeks since my arrival in Sri Lanka. I knew I was struggling, mentally as much as physically. Other people identified it more clearly than I did. People were telling me I didn't look good, that I should take a break. One morning at breakfast I thought, 'They're right, you know.' I was missing my family so much, even my dog, Spencer; deep down I knew I had to get out of there to recharge myself. But there was too much to be done for me to ease down and not pull my weight. But I was finding it very hard.

I remember little of the detail but I do remember I was walking in the village and all of a sudden my right leg felt like it had a snake unravelling inside the calf trying to strangle it. It was just excruciating pain. I remember feeling weak all over my body and, bang, lights out! I now believe it was a blood clot moving from my calf, an excruciating experience I was to feel again years later. Next thing I recall is waking up in a dreadful hospital near Galle. It wasn't until I saw the documentary for the first time that I had any concept of how bad I was and how dreadful I looked. I was quickly bundled into the back of a vehicle, put on an intravenous drip and driven to Galle with Bruce and a German doctor, Dr Stein, in the back of the wagon with me. I was so lucky that I had many good medical people around me who could act quickly.

I can remember going to the toilet at the hospital in Galle and seeing someone in a really bad way on the floor. I went back to my bed and said to Dr Stein and Sebastian, 'I can't stay here. You've got to get me out of here.' So they transferred me to the Apollo Hospital in Colombo where I was diagnosed with exhaustion, severe dehydration – basically a physical breakdown – plus back problems and, surprise, surprise, stuffed knees.

One of the volunteers, Michelle, was assigned to go to Colombo with me to make sure I got the right attention. She checked my emails and took care of any administration problems which came up from time to time, as well as making sure I got the best treatment from the best doctors and nurses. She was my conduit to the outside world.

I was in hospital for ten days and I reckon I slept for three-quarters of that time. A really touching moment was when a group of people from the village came up on the bus to visit me – and that's an eight-hour round trip. I'd never had that kind of love or concern thrown my way in my life before, outside of my family. There was Babido and her mother, Chamilla, and Chamilla's husband, plus Kumara and Toyna, and even one of the Sri Lankan senior army officers and, of course, my Italian buddy Oscar. I could see the concern and stress on Oscar's face, though, and he confessed that the village was going crazy; the realisation had hit some of the people just how little they had, despite all the work that had been done. Many felt that they had not received the assistance that others had. Plus a festering issue was that they believed there were millions of dollars on offer, but they hadn't been given their share. Oscar's concern would prove well placed.

I also received visitors from the Australian Consulate, including Diane Pearce, who was a great support to us during our stay. Mr Fernandopulle also visited, which was incredible, along with his wife and some of his senior staff. It was great that they all made the effort to see me – quite overwhelming, really.

Until I collapsed, I would call Tracey every day or every second day from my mobile phone, plus we emailed when we could. I wouldn't let on about the grim side of things, just the positive side and all the successes and satisfaction we had. I could tell she was proud of me, and pleased for me, as much as we missed each other. I had to keep it from her that I was in hospital, though; it was my way of protecting her from the dark side of the reality I was in. I didn't think I needed to burden her with what was happening to me in that 'other world' and that way I didn't have to worry about her worrying about my health, if you get what I mean. I wasn't well enough to have much of a conversation anyway in those early days of my hospitalisation and I definitely couldn't have brought myself to lie to her directly; I had done enough of that when the drugs had a hold of me. So I just didn't make contact for those ten days, which was a cruel thing to do but, I thought, the best thing to do. Tracey was obviously worried when I didn't respond to her phone calls and text messages. She ended up sending an email that said she was going to divorce me unless I got back to her. Ah, that's my Tracey!

When I got out of hospital I still didn't want her worrying, so I told her a little fib, that I'd been 'up country' where there was no communication. She wasn't happy but she seemed to accept my explanation.

I went back to Peraliya for four or five days but I still felt and looked distressed; the rest just wasn't enough to make me mentally or physically strong enough to go on. I didn't feel I was contributing properly. Chamilla said to me, 'We can see it in your eyes, we can tell you have this anguish.' And I did – the tuk-tuk/bus accident and the dead bodies, the fatal car accidents back in Perth – they all kept flashing through my mind while I was in hospital and I felt like a troubled person again after being so clear-minded and positive for so long. And I felt a desperate need to see my wife and three kids.

So I booked a flight to get me out of there. I felt terrible that I was checking out and leaving Bruce, Alison and Oscar to it. We were a diverse but dynamic foursome; we were all very different and had different strengths and weaknesses, but we gelled; we made a great team. They were probably just as exhausted as I was; we could all tell that, when we gathered and spoke about our experiences each night. Here I was, breaking the chain after nine weeks of being in the front line together and never once shirking our duties. That tortured me, but I was just too dog-tired to fight it.

Before I left I checked on the old man who was the town drunk; he was virtually ignored and shunned by everyone, including his own children. In Sri Lanka, people like him would get drunk on an alcoholic 'arak', made out of coconut. I felt I had an affinity with this old bloke, having dealt with alcoholics during my treatment back home and previously having my own problems with addiction. I'd earlier made it a priority to assign a team of four to build him a shelter, although it obviously caused surprise and jealousy from those still on the waiting list. But after seeing him sitting with ants crawling everywhere, no food and nowhere to sleep, I felt we had a responsibility to help him. The tsunami didn't discriminate against the rich or the poor and neither should we, I believed.

When I went to check on him the day before I left it was obvious he'd been drunk and his food had fallen all over the floor and that had attracted a thousand ants that were eating him alive (all he had was a straw mat to sit on). I organised for someone to make sure they sprayed his hut with insect spray. Chamilla was with me and she interpreted his words for me. He complained that his children didn't come to check on him but I could tell Chamilla didn't have a lot of sympathy for him either. 'It is not right that no one wants anything to do with him,' I argued. 'He is sick; the man is an alcoholic, he needs help. Because he is an alcoholic does not deny him the rights of every other human being. We have a responsibility to look after these sorts of people.' He died while I was away, as did the gentleman who had lost his legs; both very sad.

I wanted to keep my departure pretty quiet and told only those I felt had to know, because I realised how emotional it would be and I just didn't have the energy to go right through the village and say goodbye to everyone. But there was a poignant moment, which is portrayed in the film, where I had dropped in to say goodbye to this one family I had become close to and took Chamilla with me to translate. They were visibly very upset that I was leaving and begged me to stay; it was like I had become their security blanket. I asked

Chamilla to tell them: 'I am not the type of person to leave a job half finished, and this job is not even a quarter finished. But I am tired and I need a rest. I am not superman and not a god, I am a man.'

Chamilla responded on their behalf: 'But we see you as a god; our village people see you like that, okay?' That was pretty serious stuff; no one had ever said anything like that to me before. The mother then said in her native tongue: 'If not for the volunteers, who would have helped us? They were the ones who did everything. It is because of them that we even have a drop of water.' Chamilla added, looking deep into my eyes with real affection, 'We don't want to see you hurt; like your face, it is hurt … okay?'

I broke down and sobbed. I was just that overcome by what these people were saying to me, and also by a sense that I was letting them down. That scene was an emotional moment; it will stay with me forever. 'We are deeply saddened because he is leaving,' the mother continued as she started to cry too. Sitting next to me was their son who said, 'I am sad.' I told him, 'Don't be sad. Be happy for me. Be happy that I go see my children and my wife.' I broke down again; I just couldn't stop the tears. I felt as though I was breaking a bond with these people that was deeper than anything I had experienced outside of my own family. But I couldn't stay and help them any longer; I wasn't fit to stay.

How strange and moving it was to be farewelled so openly by the people. I had moved towns endlessly as a kid but no one had ever seemed genuinely sorry I was leaving. To see how moved these people were, and to hear what they said, was a real honour. To other people from Australia or any other country not affected by the tsunami, the places and people were just images in a TV news bulletin. For me they were personal; the people were real. I felt honoured and privileged that I had had the chance to make a difference in Sri Lanka. I was devastated that I had to leave them.

The hardest part was saying goodbye to Alison, Oscar and Bruce. I left that until last, and they could see how upset I was, so they tried to make light of the moment. Someone said, 'Donny is leaving today,' but Oscar insisted, 'No, Donny is just taking a break.' Alison said, 'Thanks for playing with us … it's been a big sand pit,' which was a pretty good line, I thought, and it got a smile out of me at least. I just said, 'As Brucey says, go easy on myself a bit, eh? Be nice to myself.' Bruce, my zen mate, was always saying that when he felt I was overextending myself.

It was a tough day in my life, and I've had plenty. When I saw those few departing minutes a couple of years later in the documentary film, I couldn't believe how sad and exhausted I looked. I appeared almost drugged as I peered out the window of the mini-van driving away. I was so blank-faced and barren of expression. I was spent inside and out and probably looked just like most of the villagers did the day I arrived.

But I wasn't finished in Peraliya, that was for sure.

8

WHEN TWO WORLDS COLLIDE

When Tracey picked me up from Sydney airport, she took one look at me and shook her head in disbelief. She said she hadn't seen me so thin and gaunt since I rolled the army Land Rover way back when she was pregnant with Cory and had spent the night in a roadside ditch before getting to hospital. I'd dropped probably twelve kilos and looked pretty shabby. I just explained to her that eating dhal and rice for a long time and working in such hot and humid conditions would do that to anyone. But while I looked very average on the outside, I felt pretty good on the inside – utterly exhausted but like I had proved something to myself and achieved something I hadn't thought I was capable of. But it didn't last long. I was home but didn't feel at home, if you know what I mean.

It wasn't until I was halfway into the two-hour car trip to Newcastle that I confessed to Tracey that I'd been in hospital and had a bit of a breakdown in Sri Lanka. She was pretty pissed off, to say the least. After all we had been through – make that all I had put her through – over all these years she didn't appreciate that I had kept such a serious thing from her. But later she understood where I was coming from. I could see no use in her worrying about me when I was so far away and there was nothing she could have done to help. That would only have made me worry more and I had enough worries of my own. But I did deceive her and that hurt Tracey, although I did it with the best of intentions.

I was still exhausted and lethargic but overjoyed at seeing Tracey and the kids. It's funny but the first impressions of being home involved the 'absolute luxuries' I'd forgotten existed – like sitting in your own air-conditioned car and a comfortable house, going to our own fridge, sleeping in our bed, hopping on the internet whenever I wanted, reading the newspaper, watching television.

I slept a lot of the first few days back. I was still pretty shattered physically but it was great to share my experiences with Tracey and the kids; the kids were fairly nonchalant, especially

Cory, but they asked questions about what I did, what it was like, what kept me busy, what I ate, where I lived and all that. I felt I was taking in more about their characteristics and was more responsive to what they were doing in their lives than I had been before. I just sat and observed them some days and had this feeling right through me of how lucky I was and appreciative that I had such a great family. I felt reborn to a degree.

Cory's football had come on in leaps and bounds, which was fantastic. The rugby league season (and his final year at high school) had begun while I was in Sri Lanka and he was playing SG Ball (under 18s) for the Newcastle Knights for a second season. His team had hardly lost a game and he was really starting to prove to Knights officials that bringing him the whole width of the continent from Perth was looking like being a good investment in their, and his, future. And Tracey, Karah and Krystal enjoyed going to watch him play as a family. Both the girls had settled well into school in the new term, which was a relief as it was naturally hard for them to move and have to make friends before Christmas. Everything in their lives seemed to be on track. The girls also had their own interests and were enjoying living in Newcastle. They were in Little Athletics and Krystal was showing keenness to go into modelling and acting; she'd done a few advertising catalogues when she was in Perth and had been picked up by an agency. Karah played netball and had been a pretty good rugby league player, too, and both the girls played 'flag belt' footy with Tracey, as well as touch football. So sport was pretty universal through our family, which was great.

I hadn't really met anyone in the few months since we'd rented a house in New Lambton, other than to say hello to the neighbours – except, that is, for David Beljaars, who I struck up a conversation with at Newcastle RSL on Anzac Day when I'd come across the year before during a visit to see Cory. Dave was the only one outside of the family who knew why I went to Sri Lanka, so he came around and we had a good chat; he was very interested in how things went and how I was. It was hard to explain what we did, what my role was and how it touched me. That's where *The Third Wave* ended up being so good when it was released; it explains our experience better than my words could and that's why I tend to loan my copy to people and say, 'Watch that and you'll understand.'

I spoke for hours and hours with Tracey, telling her of my experiences. She could see I was thinking a lot more clearly about my life, that I'd got a lot of satisfaction out of my positive role in Peraliya, and that I had finally used all the expertise I'd picked up in the army. I felt satisfied that I'd had a virtual operational deployment during which I could use some of those skills I'd trained so hard to possess, all without having to throw my ugly melon into the firing line during a war. The only overseas deployment of troops during my thirteen years in the army were to Rwanda and Namibia. Timor came just a little later – it was the first real major deployment of Australian soldiers since the Vietnam War – I mean going somewhere in large numbers where there was real ammunition and a real enemy.

The longer I stayed home during those few days, though, the more restless and uneasy I became. I'd always intended to be home only for a few weeks, to recharge my batteries so I could go back to Peraliya as soon as I was in the right physical condition. But what hit me was that it wasn't just a case of going home for some R&R, seeing my family and all would be okay. It became evident what a massive clash of worlds and cultures I had just experienced – and that I fitted into the foreign, unknown Third World better than the 'real' world I'd come from.

It didn't take long for the great pride and satisfaction I'd derived from the adventure of Peraliya to turn to a feeling of 'I'm back to my mundane life; here we go again; what is my purpose here?'. I was still in a new town where I didn't know many people and the people who did know me probably thought I was crazy to have headed off overseas by myself to help people after a tsunami. What was happening in Peraliya still played on my mind so much: what were Bruce, Oscar and Alison up to? Were this project and that project being done? Was the unrest they were so worried about getting any worse?

I look back at it now and realise that it was natural to feel down and unsettled. I had found a place in a new, very different world, and felt I'd exercised some of the skills I'd been trained for in the army – it was tough, but it was exciting; it gave me a constant adrenalin flow to feel needed and appreciated and busy. In Peraliya I'd walk around the village and everyone would say hello and show their appreciation. Suddenly, I'd walk around the streets at home and no one knew who or what I was and couldn't have cared less anyway. They were in their own relatively smug, unthreatening world, with no concept of how lucky they were. I was back to being a father and husband and I was dearly glad to see Tracey, Cory, Karah and Krystal, but I quickly started to feel inadequate again: unchallenged, unfulfilled, frustrated, anxious. And the scenes I'd witnessed in Sri Lanka started to haunt me, putting me on edge psychologically again. I started to struggle big time, knowing there was so much for me still to do back there. Being so preoccupied by that at the time, I just didn't have it in me to go out and look for some role in life back home.

I explained how I felt to Tracey and it must have been hard for her to hear her husband saying he wanted to leave her and our kids so quickly again and get back to some calamity-hit part of the world that she'd never seen and could never picture no matter how much I talked about the people and events. But she understood I had to go back there – and try to finish the job.

That was easier said than done, though, as we didn't have the $2500 airfare. So Tracey put out a group email to everyone whose address we had, asking if anyone could help to get me back to Sri Lanka. That's where an old army friend, ex-Sergeant Major Craig 'Shorty' Coleman from Brisbane, came to the rescue. He worked in a personnel management agency that sent skilled workers to Afghanistan and Iraq for close body security work and also ex-army engineers for on-the-ground infrastructure work. He responded and said he wanted to help get me back to Peraliya and his company paid for my airfare, which I was grateful for. Shorty had been a real mentor to me when I was in the army, coaching me in touch footy, of which he was quite a player himself. I owe him a lot. We were all pretty sharp touch players in those days; I remember fondly the good times playing competitive sport and the camaraderie that would build up between people. We were all so fit, too, and we played the game hard; I loved it.

So my visit to Australia lasted less than two weeks. It was hard to say goodbye to Tracey and the kids again, even though they'd become used to it over the years with my army exercises and stints in hospital trying to sort myself out. But I just knew I had to get back to Sri Lanka and finish what I'd set out to do.

I was back in Peraliya by mid-April. Kumara and Dinesh came to Colombo airport to meet me and it was great to see their faces. I was almost shaking with excitement as we drove down the main Galle Road. There had been a lot of mopping up and a lot of construction in the towns and villages along the way, but there was still a lot to do. It's funny – we had driven that way out to the airport when I went home but I hadn't noticed the progress, which shows I was either asleep or so 'spaced out' with exhaustion I just didn't see it or certainly didn't take it in. This time I felt energised, upbeat and keen to see everyone, and I was much more aware of what was around me.

When I arrived in Peraliya, I felt like the Pied Piper; all the kids gathered around yelling, 'Donny's back, Donny's back.' I will never forget that welcome; so many people milling around, fifty to sixty people with beaming smiles, patting me on the back, wanting to hug me. I learned some of them had been crying for me that I wasn't there; that blew me away.

In the eighteen or so hours between leaving Newcastle and arriving at Peraliya, it was like I was transformed from one identity to another – Donny, the face in the crowd who kept to himself, to Donny with a slouch hat, walking stick and orange vest – the inspiring hero of the people. That was the role that made me feel worthwhile and fulfilled even though I had just left all the comforts of home and an affluent society to come to a tsunami-devastated Third World environment. But that had become 'me'.

9

A VILLAGE UNDER SIEGE

Peraliya had changed in the three weeks or so I'd been absent in the Colombo hospital and back in Australia. And not for the better. The evil element had grown bigger. A dangerous level of anarchy had taken over the place. As Oscar had told me in Colombo, some people realised they still had nothing, and they resented that. Those villagers turned on the people who had helped them the most and given them what they did have: the volunteers. Bit by bit I learned of a place gone feral in just a few short weeks, a place that had turned to widespread tension, confrontation and violence. Even my trusted right-hand man Kumara had been swept up by the festering ill-content and turned on the helpers from outside. Peraliya and surrounding villages had gone crazy to the extent that Alison, Oscar, Bruce and their valued colleagues who had joined us felt like packing up and walking away.

I don't know how many times I'd said, 'Desperate people will do desperate things.' Sadly, it had become a fulfilled prophecy – and I hadn't been there to try to stem the infection of discontent.

It broke my heart to find that Kumara and Dr Stein, who was one of the most placid people I came across during our Sri Lankan mission, were at each other's throats, screaming in front of a hostile crowd as if someone had lit a fuse, and the sleepy, friendly village of Peraliya had erupted into a hotbed of uncontrollable emotion. Suspicion and deceit among certain villagers were rife, and a murder and several stabbings had occurred at the height of the nightmare. I didn't see the ugly confrontations for myself until I watched them, captured vividly, in *The Third Wave*, and I believe that footage showed only the tip of the iceberg. In one way I was glad I missed the drama; in another, I wished I had been there because I felt I might have done a lot towards restoring calm as a trusted middle-man.

To see Kumara shouting his grievances, including disputing whether the medical centre should continue to exist in the library, and Dr Stein yelling: 'Go – just go,' as he angrily waved his arms, showed me two things: one, that the evil element had infiltrated to such a degree that even Kumara got swept up in it (no doubt he was being used by the belligerent bad element to air their grievances to the volunteers); and, secondly, that the desperate plight of Kumara and loss of his family, and the anger and anxiety he had inside, just boiled over. We had done everything we could for all the people of Peraliya, but it wasn't enough, and people just got desperate. The realisation hit home that they had nothing, and some were jealous of those who did have something provided by us, as little as that might have been.

We didn't know who had what before we arrived, or what status or hierarchy existed between different families. We just tried to help whoever we could and as many as we could, with no discrimination between colour, race, religion, wealth or anything else. We had no manual, no guidelines to follow, but if it wasn't for us maybe nothing at all would have been done for these people. Administering aid to such a large number of people was hard, so we took every case on its merit. Even with the temporary shelters, it was too difficult for me to decide what order to allocate them in, so in the end I handballed it to the chief and said, 'You decide who is really in need,' and he would consult the village elders and come back with a list. I think we finally did them alphabetically.

Three and a half months after the tsunami most of the people were still unable to resume the fishing industry that had sustained them for so long, there were few houses, they were short on food, and still didn't have a fully functional school to send their children to. They felt desperate. There were two reported suicide attempts during the couple of weeks I was away, including a teenage boy who threw himself in front of a train. Somehow he survived and was very fortunate he had such good medical help on tap in the village, with Dr Stein taking particularly good care of him, I was told. The boy's father was wheelchair-bound and the boy and his brother had kept his head above the water as it rose after the tsunami. But his father was in and out of hospital with terrible bedsores and infections and didn't lead much of a life. Unfortunately he died a few months after we'd finally left; I think the local medical system let him down without the volunteers and our medical staff around.

A particular group of women always tried to cause trouble. I'm not sure if it was sparked by past grievances or whether they were just envious and resentful that others who they had some beef with appeared to be favoured in the rebuilding process. There was obvious jealousy that some had been seen as receiving help and others not, and there was obviously a village status issue too: some who might have had a nice home and a greater standing within the village social system, were still waiting in line and struggling with nothing while others who may have been beneath them previously at least had shelters.

Those people didn't trust anyone. They liked to create all these conspiracies and make up ill-founded stories of others getting grand handouts of money or goods, which were vicious and untrue. And they would lie for their own benefit. As Alison said on her website, it became a bit like the book and movie *The Lord of the Flies*, in which a bunch of schoolboys stranded on an island turn on themselves in the most savage way. And many of the villagers genuinely believed we had wads of money to hand around and were angry, and very understandably, that they had seen none of the reported $2.18 billion in aid money that was supposed to be flooding into Sri Lanka. If they trusted anyone from our group, I'd like to think it was me. I'd busted my guts to give them what I promised without fear or favour; if I couldn't provide what they wanted I'd tell them I couldn't. I naturally had favourites among the villagers, like Kumara. I wouldn't provide him and his family with money or resources that I wouldn't give to others, but I was happy to take him for a meal or to the swimming pool at my hotel in Hikkaduwa just to give him a break from the grind of the work and some little luxury in life.

Alison bore the brunt of the unrest. She received several death threats, some in writing thrown through the window of the library, while drunks would tell her bombs had been planted under the makeshift hospital. She also received verbal threats to her face, basically telling her to 'be careful' as the villagers were about to take things into their own hands. And having to treat some nasty knife wounds sustained by locals who were attacked by rival groups or gangs, and knowing that people were quite willing to kill others over a dispute, made her believe the threats were real. A boy was shot one day out the front of his place; someone stuck a 9mm pistol to his head but no one was game to identify who the assailant was.

The Sri Lankan police had set up a station on the edge of the village to ensure they had a strong presence. I'm pretty sure Mr Fernandopulle was responsible for that after he visited and saw the potential for trouble. But even the police had problems coping with the antagonism and growing violence. I'm not sure whether they ever arrested anyone over the murder, but they probably didn't. I can't say the policing techniques of the local force were like what we are used to back home, something I learned first-hand. One evening I had seen a guy hanging around Casa Lanka looking suspicious. We knew him; we called him 'Milko' because he would ask for money to buy milk for his children. It seemed more than coincidental that we had several items stolen from our rooms that night, including a laptop computer belonging to the English photographer Juliet Coombe. Oscar, Juliet and I reported the thefts to the Hikkaduwa police station and I told them that Milko had been hanging around. Within an hour they had him at the station, while we were still there filling out our reports, and I never want to see or hear what happened next ever again in my life. The police beat the absolute crap out of this guy and forced him to make a confession. I felt absolutely gutted; I'd seen him hanging around and he had to be the main suspect but I didn't see him steal anything (although I suspect he did). Whether he was guilty or innocent, he wasn't going to leave there without a confession!

A very different story was that of Buddhika, a very talented artist who we naturally all took to. One day he told Alison he and his sister couldn't go to school any more because they had to fish to help get money in for his family. Alison thought that would be a tragedy and that he should continue at school and use his talents. So she gave the family some money, donated by a friend from the US on the condition it was used on one particular family. They were one of the poorer families and had lost their boat and home. Alison's action allowed both the children to stay at school and the family to keep feeding them. It was one of those hard discretionary decisions we had to make.

Another time Alison was accused of providing $500 to an antique dealer from Ambalangoda who had lost his store in the tsunami and had no income. The word got around about her alleged gesture and there was holy hell to pay from the group who were already on the warpath. The chief took her to task because he felt she'd allocated money to someone without his permission and, to make it worse, it was someone from outside the village. He accused Alison of giving money to the 'thieves and whores' of the country. Alison gave no cash to the antique dealer. This was typical of the unfounded rumours that would travel around the village. She did provide him with a tent. If we visited someone in their tent or shelter just to say 'hi' and check how they were going, a rumour would spread through the village that we had given them hundreds or even thousands of dollars. It was like Big Brother was watching our every move.

Trivial things became big issues, like the fact that we spent $1000 of donated money on brick-making machines and mosquito nets, which were both very important and integral to the work we were doing to rebuild their village and give them some quality of life. Yet when we handed out clothes and mosquito nets, we would almost get our arms clawed off in the desperate rush of hands grabbing whatever we had on offer.

Alison did not deserve the anger and lies that some dealt her. So many people who came to Peraliya were only interested in helping. We showed no favouritism. Maybe we had spoiled too many people in Peraliya: they had come to rely on us, knowing they *could* rely on us. Alison's spirit always looked unshakable to me, but it became very fragile during this time. She commented on the website: 'At night I cry alone in my bed. I am just trying to help them. I have given my heart, my soul and every cent I own to these people. This trip has left me confused about mankind and how cruel and how kind we can be to each other.'

The people of Peraliya were aware that they'd received far more assistance and far quicker rebuilding than any other place in the Galle-to-Colombo strip, but it was like a handout to them and I worked on the principle that we were there to give a hand *up* rather than a hand *out*. In the end it was a case of anything that needed fixing, get Donny and he will 'make it good' – that was a common term they used, 'You make it good' – whether it was a small repair job or repairing wells so they had water. And that was the hardest thing to get through; people might not have any running water yet but they had four walls and a roof while others didn't have even that. We had to convince people that we were doing the best we could. I must have said a thousand times a day, 'Be patient … you must be patient,' but in the end they got so frustrated they ran out of patience. And we didn't have the money or resources to rebuild their houses like they were before, or bring back the lives they had lost. A lot of their frustration centred on the 'where's the money?' argument. So many people had heard of these billions of dollars that were supposed to have come into the country; in the end they were accusing each other of stealing funds or even us for spending it on ourselves. The fact was, we were spending our own money on them, and we didn't have much of that!

It was so sad that Kumara and Chinthu, who I had built such a good relationship with, went a bit loose during the period I was away. One of the first things I did on my return was to take Kumara aside and, with the help of an interpreter, explain to him that he had to calm down. He was going through his grief and we had to understand that, but I told him the antagonism had to stop. I said, 'I know it is hard for you but if this continues it's not going to help anyone at all.' He just needed a bit of guidance and for someone to tell him we cared. Here was a guy who wouldn't leave my side before and was so loyal and hardworking for our cause, but in the end he felt helpless and frustrated like everyone else. I don't think Dr Stein realised he was unwell or what he was going through after losing his wife and children and never being able to find their bodies.

The ringleader of the discontent was a woman who is often seen confronting us with complaints in the film – even Sunil, the camera operator, was targeted for deciding to assist with the making of the film rather than getting his hands dirty with the manual work. He explained later that he wanted to remain neutral and that was a good way of doing that. One distressing event, and again I only witnessed this in the film because I was in Australia at the time, was when this woman threatened Alison and Oscar, saying they had a problem and if they didn't do something about it others would, meaning the rebel group in the village. Their way of 'doing something' would have meant violence and mass revolt, it seems.

Unbelievably, even Chamilla got caught up in the revolt. She was such a loving, kind and even-tempered lady who we took everywhere to act as our interpreter, yet she was accused by this group of lying when she interpreted what they said to us or when relaying our views back to them, changing the meanings for her own convenience. One day when she had been taken to task verbally by this one evil woman (shown graphically in *The Third Wave*), she started pointing and shouting at Oscar, claiming it was his 'fucking fault' for giving the women money because they then caused trouble by saying they had received nothing. It was the only time I knew her to swear. Kumara snapped at her, saying she should be beaten for speaking so defiantly and pointing at Oscar. I had never seen Chamilla rattled at any other time, so that showed how volatile everything had become. Alison was angry and upset, too, and it took a lot to rattle her. Bruce was level-headed, always seeing the middle ground of everything, always the calming influence.

Apparently while I was away in Australia things became so bad that a meeting of the volunteer group was held to determine whether the situation had become too unstable and dangerous for them to carry on. They discussed the idea of explaining to the villagers that, because of their complaining and threats and the resulting fear, the volunteers would have to leave. Typically, Bruce acted as the diplomatic arbiter and calmed the situation, saying there was no benefit in lodging ultimatums. He reminded them that it was a small minority stirring up trouble and they needed to reiterate to the locals that they were not trying to change their lives or their systems but to give them the infrastructure to get back on track with their lives.

They decided to have a meeting with the villagers and four or five times as many turned up than would usually attend a meeting. The locals were asked whether they wanted a medical centre, as there had been so much bitching about using the school library as the centre, but when the idea of closing the centre was put to them, they weren't happy. They didn't want to lose the medical centre, they just wanted us to get alternative premises for it, which eventually happened. It seems a lot of the claims by the rebel women 'on behalf of everyone in the village' were bullshit; there was no consensus at all.

On top of all that drama while I was back in Australia, there was the panic one night when another tsunami warning was relayed to the village. Probably once a week someone who was drunk at the time would scream, 'Tsunami!' I remember the first time, it was like a stampede: people running inland in sheer, blind panic. You could see the terror in their eyes. Next door at Telwatta there was a temple on higher ground and people would run the two kilometres there. Each time it would take us nearly an hour to restore calm. Children wouldn't come out again, they were so petrified, so we had to tempt them back to the village with the promise of ice blocks or ice creams.

On 28 March at about 10.30 pm, the warning was for real. Bulletins had gone out all over the world about an offshore earthquake and the possibility of another tsunami hitting South-East Asia. Alison and Oscar received calls from Germany and Italy, and James, the British journalist who had helped us, sent a warning saying 'huge earthquake … tsunami warning … head for higher ground'. In Australia I had also heard about the warning and sent my text message to Peraliya, too, as the world stood by for another potential disaster. The remaining volunteers, and there were probably only six or seven by then, would have liked to have organised a controlled evacuation but that just wasn't possible considering the circumstances and the fear that still existed after the previous tsunami.

Many people fled on foot to higher ground in the dark with their children in their arms, desperate not to lose more of their beloved young ones. Others tied ropes to the top of coconut trees, ready to climb above the expected giant wave. The volunteers rode through the village providing updates on what was happening. There was reasonable calm but mass anxiety.

Everyone waited nervously for hours before international

A VILLAGE UNDER SIEGE

text messages came in stating that there was no tsunami; certainly there was a quake that measured 8.7 on the Richter scale, centred off the coast of Indonesia about twenty-five kilometres south-east of Banda Aceh and only 160 kilometres from the Boxing Day earthquake epicentre, so it was right to have been concerned. Tremors were felt in Indonesia, Thailand, Malaysia and Singapore, but as Alison, Oscar, Bruce and the village leaders looked out to the horizon under the moonlight and through night goggles, there was no upheaval in the ocean. However, thirteen people were reported to have died in Sri Lanka in motor accidents or from heart attacks while frantically trying to escape to higher ground. About three hundred died in Indonesia as a result of the violent tremors caused by the earthquake.

Another thing that must have really frustrated the villagers, too, was that quite a few boats, funded by Larry Buck and his group Bread for a Hungry World, had arrived but we were unable to source any motors or nets for them to be utilised. They sat there, teasing the local fishermen, really, for weeks and weeks. All the stocks of nets were exhausted after the tsunami and in the end we sourced a few from Scotland and had them shipped over but we were never able to get hold of any motors before I left.

I certainly missed an uneasy time in Peraliya. I returned after the rebellion, when a reasonable level of calm had been restored. Then there was a storm of a different kind: a lot of people began protesting in the streets of Hikkaduwa and Galle demanding to know the location of the $2.18 billion aid money; there was little evidence of any of it reaching those parts of Sri Lanka. Oscar even went to United Nations office and to the government to ask where the money was. Mr Fernandopulle had no idea where it had gone. 'Someone took the money and must be living a jolly life somewhere,' he said; not a bad line. He was virtually accusing people of impropriety. When the mayor of Galle was interviewed he said, 'We don't know where the account is; we don't know where the bank is; we don't know where the money is!'

People who had had houses within 100 metres of the coastline had also started to protest in the streets, asking why they had had to move and where was their aid after being dumped in the middle of nowhere with little infrastructure. So unrest was growing quickly. The locals were definitely feeling that all the great promises of international help were something of a con, and they had been let down. Don't get me wrong, most were very appreciative of what we had done for them and even the troublemakers later conceded that. Human emotion is a powerful thing – good and bad, positive and negative – and at distressing times it tends to magnify itself considerably.

I'd like to think my return at the end of that difficult period helped calm things a little bit further and gave some reassurance to the people that they had a friend, and a 'straight down the middle' contributor back to help Alison, Oscar, Bruce and the others whose motives should never, ever have been questioned. Figuratively, there were some bridges to mend, while physically there was even more to do.

10

THE SECOND COMING

The storm of emotion died down somewhat in Peraliya, the monsoons had passed and we were able to focus our energies back where they were most needed: improving the lives of those around us. As Alison kept saying, 'Look at the bigger picture,' and the big picture was that there was much still to be done. People were still living in the many tents and temporary shelters that had been erected, some of them housing eight children and four adults in one room, and some still didn't have water or electricity connected.

A funny episode (although it wasn't at the time) happened after it was decided to plant 500 new coconut trees to replace the many that were destroyed in the tsunami and to enhance the look of the village, an exercise Bruce and Irishman Jeff, a wonderful worker who stayed quite a while, were proudly in charge of. You wouldn't bloody believe it, but quite a few of them were pulled out in the middle of the night by locals who had been drinking! They were replanted and this time the inebriated culprits left them alone.

We were also able to put in place Sri Lanka's first tsunami warning system. Who would have thought the country's first such warning station would be located at Peraliya, which wasn't even on the tourist map? An internet link was established to receive regular information and it is now manned by local labour. It had an opening ceremony, organised by Dr Novil, the Sinhalese doctor who used to travel from Colombo down the coast to dedicate his time and expertise free of charge a few days a week. A nice touch was that a projector and big screen were organised to show the movie *Finding Nemo* – it was the first time many of the children had seen moving images.

The centre has grown to be far more than somewhere that tsunamis, earthquakes or hurricanes can be detected 24/7. I think a lot of funding support came from Alison's parents and friends at the Cronulla Rotary Club, and from a woman in New Zealand. It now has a free, privately run ambulance service (one ambulance) and a public library with a computer for use. The fear of a tsunami hitting again remained for a long time, and the people feel reassured by the information available at the centre, which is relayed right along the coast to appointed families who have telephones. Speakers have also been mounted around the village so that announcements can be made quickly and loudly.

A nice thing that happened while I was away was that the four of us received Humanitarian Awards from the Sri Lankan government, organised by Mr Fernandopulle, and were given plaques as mementos; it was much appreciated recognition.

Oscar loved his football – soccer (well, he is Italian) – and started coaching a team in Hikkaduwa, as well as playing in the side when he could, which was a great release for him and something he really enjoyed. Not so much fun was that we were still recovering dead bodies right into April, three and a half months after the tsunami hit.

After having taken photos of all the children for their ID tags, Bruce arranged to take photos of all the families so they had some personal possession as a keepsake of the year. They would be posted on the walls of their homes, along with the rare photos they may have saved of their family members who were taken by the two monstrous waves. I gave Kumara a photograph of my family and, in a real heart-rending moment for me, he blew it up and superimposed the faces of his family onto it and gave it to me as a gift. It is a possession I hold very, very dearly. To comprehend that my family was at home safe while all his family members were dead, that really hit home to me and made me even more thankful for what I had.

We were able to hand the library back to the villagers to use for its original purpose, as a reading place, thanks to a new medical centre being constructed and stocked, due largely to the dedication of Dr Thomas Stein, that wonderful man from Hamburg in Germany, and funding from the Deutsche Bank. Bruce used his contacts to get a complete set of instruments (guitars and drum kit) from the Canadian band Rush to give to the local band who'd had all their instruments washed away in the tsunami.

Although we'd come a long way in a few months, and there was still much to do, we were quickly confronting the realisation that there wasn't much more we could contribute with the resources we had. The flood of volunteers had come and gone, which was to be expected as many had to get on with their own lives, and I guess the bureaucratic nonsense had grown in regard to aid money and the rights and territories of the aid organisations who, according to all the reports I have since read, were becoming more and more frustrated by the lack of detail and follow through on the part of the Sri Lankan government.

I was back only six weeks when we decided, quite spontaneously, really, that it was time to leave. As Bruce said, 'It's time to give the village back to the people.' I wouldn't say we'd finished the job, because the job was a long way short of being completed, but we just thought it was right – although Alison and Oscar did return for quite a while, and others I'll tell you about later devoted a lot more time over the next few years to the village we had adopted. We had a meeting and decided we had put enough in place for them to move forward with new hope. The school had been reopened, a new medical centre built and stocked and boats had been bought from several generous sources. A bakery had been built to replace the old one; those brick machines were squeezing out some income as builders from other towns placed orders from them. When someone in the group mentioned that we should be thinking about getting back to our own lives, there was an all-round nod of agreement. We were exhausted, we'd gone through the entire spectrum of emotions and it just felt right. But we all knew what a wrench to our hearts it would be.

Decision made, we did not want to prolong the big farewell. 'Let's just do it,' we thought. We relayed our decision to the chief and to those close to us, and I think we were out of the place within five or six days. We had a wonderful farewell event and the *poya* (full moon) celebration fell within the last forty-eight hours before we departed, too, so it was a pretty special goodbye the village put on for us; very emotional for us all. They provided a big feast and all prayed for us, then had a presentation to the 'original four', which was just so touching I still get tears in my eyes when I watch it on *The Third Wave* and hear the piano soundtrack in the background, and then see the image of us saying goodbye on the last night.

Dr Novil was the master of ceremonies. He was such a wonderful, kind-hearted soul – one of many I met. Each of us received a certificate and a garland which was draped around our necks by one of the children, and an individual honorary title was bestowed on us. Alison was named 'The Nightingale of Peraliya' after 'the Lady with the Lamp', famous wartime nurse Florence Nightingale. Oscar was tagged 'The Visionary of Peraliya'; and Bruce was anointed 'The Master of Peraliya' and received a big hug of appreciation from the village chief. I loved my title – 'The Shepherd of Peraliya' – which intimated that the flock followed me, that I was a leader. It could easily have been 'The Shithead of Peraliya' or something like that. A garland was presented to all the other volunteers who had come to the village, too, and they deserved one.

We went back to Hikkaduwa and had a farewell dinner together, 'The Fab Four' plus a few other volunteers who had become dear friends. I didn't know how to feel as we were preparing to leave: happy or sad, glad or mad. A lot had gone into those five months – so much human emotion and blood, sweat and tears. I put myself out there big time, threw myself into that project more than anything I had done in my life. It was an intense, relentless, heart-wrenching, emotional five-month period and to come to the realisation that it was over was almost overwhelmingly hard to deal with. As Bruce said, our group dynamics had been pulled in all directions and we got through it. We were very proud of what we did, and we knew it was better than what a lot of trained, well-funded aid organisations had done elsewhere.

To think we were just four people who stopped by and set up a first-aid station out of a hired van on 10 January and, here we were, at the end of May, with tens of thousands of patients having been treated. We had built about 500 permanent homes along the coast; put some infrastructure into the evacuee camp at Alluthawalla; repaired an orphanage at Galle; sent dozens of independent volunteers to many other villages along the coastline to help rebuild lives; had over 200 volunteer staff give us their time and their hearts; had aid groups from several countries come and help, plus church and charity groups; and had many, many individuals donate money to our efforts at such a tiny dot on the map of the vast area affected by the tsunami. It's incomprehensible to think a chance meeting at Colombo airport and the great determination and unyielding loyalty of Oscar, Alison, Bruce and I could create something like that.

We couldn't help everyone, we couldn't please everyone, we couldn't do everything right and we certainly didn't. But our intentions and motives were nothing but pure and unrelenting. We still can't comprehend exactly what the people of all the affected countries went through, to have the lives of so many of their friends and families, and the livelihoods of those who survived, taken away from them. We saw them grieve and cry and dust themselves off and try to get on with their lives, and we tried to understand and make them feel we were there for them. But ultimately we were going to go home to our unaffected families and friends and our much more affluent lives, so we couldn't totally identify with them. But we went as close as we possibly could.

It was so sad that, as Alison walked to the chief's house in those final couple of days, a small delegation of the 'evil element' women stood in her way, smiling smugly. Alison asked them why they were so nasty to her, why they persecuted her despite all she had done, and they said, 'You never helped us.' They knew that was a lie. 'I looked at them in shock as I thought of the personal things we have done for them over the months from medical to mozzie nets, toilets, clean water, clothes, food, flasks to rebuilding their entire village and fortunes,' Alison recorded on her website diary. 'I wanted to cry out in pain to make them see; I wanted to pry open their eyes with crowbars because I couldn't listen to their lies any longer. But something inside me said "look at the big picture". I couldn't give them the one thing they really wanted and that was their children or their husbands and if they were angry at me for that, then it was okay.'

Saying goodbye to the villagers and all the familiar sights was sad enough. There were a lot of tears. To say goodbye to our own group, one by one, was tougher; these were people I had learned to admire more than just about anyone I had met in my life. That was cutting the umbilical cord in a sense – it was the end of that incredible episode of our lives together; certainly not the end of wonderful friendships, but of the experience we all shared together. But we knew we'd be together again – we'd vowed to have a reunion in Hikkaduwa on the first anniversary of the tsunami.

Oscar and I had our moments during those few months in Peraliya, I have to admit that. We think differently on some things and don't always see eye to eye because we are such different people, but I still think fondly of him and greatly admire what he did and how he worked hard on projects with so much Italian passion; he gave so much to the children. He knew we needed someone to be in control, to chair our meetings, to ensure things across all areas of the operation were done, and he threw himself into that role.

Bruce – old Mr Zen – had to have been a guru or a maharishi in a previous life. He was the comforting influence always, a wonderful, warm-hearted ally and the close mate I needed during those unrelenting days. He was the jack-of-all-trades who could always see the big picture, the end result, the need to keep in perspective who we were, what we needed to do, and that we were different people with different dynamics and it was only natural we were going to get frustrating hurdles thrown at us each day. He kept reassuring us we had a job to do and we were doing it bloody well on any level of assessment.

Alison? Just so resilient, so benevolent, so focused. She probably had the toughest job in that she saw more death, more injury and more misfortune than the rest of us. She was the focal point for those who wanted sympathy as much as any medical treatment, and was also in the front line of people's hostility. But she never caved in, not in front of anyone else at least, although sometimes I heard her cry at night.

And so we all departed to different parts of the world and very different lives to the one we had shared in that small, destroyed village. The four of us – Alison Thompson (originally from Cronulla, Australia) and Oscar Gubernati (originally from Palermo, Italy) from New York City, Bruce French from Telluride, Colorado, in the US, and Donny Paterson from Newcastle, New South Wales, Australia – are inextricably linked forever. If I hadn't witnessed it, I would not have believed what we did was possible. Alison and Oscar were only back in the Big Apple for a few weeks;

they couldn't settle and returned to Peraliya for a further seven months. Bruce almost immediately headed off on a world tour with Pearl Jam as the band's private chef. I started to get more involved in my sports training and first-aid duties back in rugby league in Newcastle, plus some charity work.

A few of the volunteers stayed or returned for varying lengths of time. And Alison continued to encourage people to go to Peraliya or any part of Sri Lanka to help. As she said: 'It's just about getting your hands dirty, that's why I really believe anyone can become a volunteer. You don't need many skills to hand out water or give someone a hug; you just need a little love and a whole lot of heart.' That's so true.

I had become so immersed in the culture, the relative poverty and their desperate situation, and now I had to confront returning to 'my' existence with infinitely more wealth, food and comforts, and a more gentle climate. I felt so much apprehension about how the villagers would get on after we'd left but I had to move forward.

I felt really calm, though, clear and satisfied that I had proved I could be a good person, that I could do worthy things, and I was determined that that good person was going to prosper in my own world. I was able to let go of so much of the anger and bitterness I had been carrying around since 1997. Just a few months earlier I had still felt incompetent and weak, which was

A tightknit group during a time of need. From left: Sunil, Stefan, Alison, Bruce, the chief, me and Oscar.

New York, New York ... an overawed Aussie on 42nd Street. Unreal!

Alison, Bruce and me in the back of a stretch limo on the way to the Cannes Film Festival.

Red-carpet treatment: Bruce, Alison, me, Petra and Oscar at Cannes.

A surprise visit from Brad Pitt was another exciting memory from Cannes.

Sean Penn and me in his penthouse. What a week!

The view from the penthouse I shared with Sean Penn in Cannes: not a bad outlook!

Facing the media at the Cannes Film Festival.

It was great to see Chinthu when I returned to Peraliya in 2009, although the innocence had gone from his eyes.

The big Buddha that stands at Peraliya as a memorial to the tsunami victims.

The Shepherd of Peraliya and the Chief of Peraliya.

When I returned in 2009, it blew me away to see the new school buildings all around the old library and smaller school block; those two were among the only buildings left standing when I was in the village in 2005.

The memorial to those who died in the *Queen of the Sea* tragedy.

Karah met Alison and enjoyed some of the local hospitality when she accompanied me to Peraliya over Christmas 2005.

Cory, Karah and Krystal in 2006.

My older sister, Christeen, and me.

Proud grandparents: Tracey and me with Tayah.

Below: The other 'Fab Four' who have stood by me, in a family shot taken at our home in Newcastle. From left: Cory, Karah, Krystal, Tracey and me.

The Shepherd of Peraliya.

Courtesy Alison Thompson

how I had been made to feel since a decade earlier when I was spat out by the army. I couldn't run even two kilometres because of my knees and had had to keep pumping prescribed painkillers into me (tramadol, Panadeine Forte and Norspan patches, which were changed weekly) just to walk around the village every day, but how could I be incompetent and weak after what I had just achieved? It was truly a 'light bulb' experience for me.

Those poor people of Peraliya, the good and the evil, did as much for me as I did for them – even though they'll never know that. But *I* do, and that's what counts. The candle that had lain dormant inside me for so long had been lit again. If that had not happened at that particular time of my life, I shudder to think what the consequences would have been. Those people taught me what was important in life. I'd woken up to the fact that I should appreciate being able to turn a switch and have the power come on, or turn a tap and have water come out. I didn't have to worry about a roof over my head, or living in poverty; I had a loving wife and family and so much more. I had been blinded to that, but the people of Peraliya helped me open my eyes.

That experience was a wake-up call for Donny Thomas Paterson and I wasn't ever going to forget that. I wouldn't, I couldn't, let myself betray the honour the poor people of that little corner of Sri Lanka had given me – 'The Shepherd of Peraliya'.

11

NEW MAN IN MY OLD WORLD

I felt alive again, and I felt excited about being alive, excited about what I had done. I never realised this situation would change my life so much for the better. But I was conscious of the warning signs from my past life too. As satisfying as our efforts in Peraliya were, it was also a traumatic experience and I had put my body and mind through the grinder. I needed to unload all the grief and anguish that was inside me from what I had witnessed and felt.

I told Tracey I wasn't feeling real good psychologically and I was going to take the bull by the horns and get some professional 'debriefing'. I booked myself into Lingard Private Hospital for some psychological assessment and trauma counselling. As I've said before, I'd learned that the opportunity to share my grief and anguish to someone else can provide a massive release and this time I knew I needed it. I wasn't going to allow myself to suppress all my emotions again, to get down to a deep depression again. I was at the clinic for a week and had some expert counselling, did rapid eye movement therapy and psychotherapy where they make you comfortable in a safe room and take you through the experience deep in your subconscious. It is tough – just ask anyone who has gone through trauma counselling – but you're so relieved when you unload it. That all helped enormously in allowing me to get on with my life with a clear head, and after that week I felt ready to be the new Donny Paterson and make sure my experience in Sri Lanka had a lasting effect on me as well as the people of Peraliya.

Soon after I went down and joined Newcastle Wests rugby league club as head trainer for the juniors. The current club secretary, Mick Weston, has been very supportive of me, which I appreciate. Sports training is what I like to do most. I love the camaraderie and the enthusiasm of the young players, and their parents really appreciate what I do. The following season I became involved in the under-17 development squad of the Newcastle Knights, which put me in the picture for further advancement. And with other volunteer activities my days became quite full and productive.

The Newcastle Herald did a couple of stories on my adventures as a few people back home learned of what I had done. I'm not sure how the word got out but I also heard from the local television station, NBN. It was a bit bizarre but I got used to a bit of media coverage and felt that, hopefully, my story might inspire a few people to do that little extra for worthy causes. I don't expect people to go 15,000 miles to make a difference – there is so much you can do in your own community.

The good thing about the second half of 2005, when all the family was reunited, was that Cory's football came on in leaps and bounds. He played SG Ball (under 18s) again and was promoted to the Jersey Flegg (under 20s) when the SG Ball competition finished (the Flegg competition went two months longer). He was also chosen for the Australian Schoolboys side and played two 'Tests' against the Junior Kiwis. They won the first and lost the second, and when I look back now it was a pretty big honour for Cory to play in that company – from the Australian team these players have already become regular first graders in the NRL: Cory, Jarrod Mullen, Mitch Aubusson, Darius Boyd, Michael Jennings, Joel Moon, Mitchell Pearce and David Taylor; in fact Pearce, Jennings and Boyd have played State of Origin. The Kiwis had Greg Eastwood, Sonny Fa'ai, Isaac Luke, Frank-Paul Nuuausala, Sam Rapira, Setaimata Sa, Ben Te'o and Cooper Vuna.

In 2006 Cory played for the Knights in the Jersey Flegg (under 20s) competition and the Knights were beaten in the grand final 22–20 by St George Illawarra after being minor premiers, but individually he had a great season. He was picked in the New South Wales under 19s then in the junior Kangaroos, the Australian under-19s team, which was a massive honour.

Certainly, I had to reacquaint myself with my children and I was determined to become a better father. They got through relatively unscathed when I was ill, and I think that was because we had been honest and open about it and Tracey had been such a great mother to them. We never tried to hide my problems and Tracey never tried to hide me like my father did with my mother; we took it head-on as a family. And I believe having that family around me saved me. I would not have made it without them – in fact I don't think I would be here now; I would be dead or in a mental institution with a fried brain.

I knew I had a lot of catching up to do after being away a fair bit while in the army, either on duty or later when I was in hospital for long stints, and then spending almost five months in Sri Lanka when the kids were in their teens and at an important stage of their development. When I was going through the bad phases of my addiction I was a terrible father – a 'deadbeat dad', as they say. I was hopeless physically, spiritually and emotionally; I wasn't there for them and that hurts a lot. I remember lashing out towards the kids both physically and verbally; it was like there were two of me, Donny and Druggie Donny, as Tracey called that other side of me. There would be stretches when I was right then stretches when I'd fall down again and something would trigger me off and I'd have to get away from my demons.

When I came home from Sri Lanka it was clear in my mind that I wanted to feel good about myself so I could be a better person for them. As someone once said, 'You have to love yourself before you can truly love someone else.' I learned how to love myself from my experience in Sri Lanka. My perceived failure as a soldier really drove me into a deep depression; that was the phase of my life that I was determined would be over, although it is only natural when you suffer from clinical depression that there are always going to be some bad days. It's hard having a small family with no cousins around and none of Tracey's family nearby, and me only having Christeen, who has no children, in Sydney. So it has been hard for the kids and they needed two loving, supportive parents.

With the reunion of the volunteers on the first anniversary of the tsunami, I was away from the family again for four weeks through Christmas, New Year and our nineteenth wedding anniversary, which wasn't much fun for Tracey. But I got to take Karah, who was then fifteen, with me. It was pretty special to take her inside the other world I had lived in during those months away and to give her some perspective on how fortunate our lives were. I introduced her to a lot of people from the village and naturally to the volunteers who had gone back for the reunion. Chinthu, Kumara and Dinesh were delighted to meet her.

Alison and Oscar had been back there from July to early November but they made one more trip to honour our 'date'. So did Bruce, James, Dr Sebastian Pluese, some other volunteers I got to know well – Peter Nossiter and his wife and son Rob – and Rob's girlfriend, Jo. I was emotional as usual when we first met up – but I took the mickey out of everyone, too, don't worry. As I gave Alison a hug Oscar yelled, 'That's the go; that's the gooooooo!' Ah, the old catchcry will never be forgotten. It was emotional enough catching up with the other volunteers but to see the villagers again, and the children running around yelling out, 'Donny, Donny,' was a bit overwhelming. I felt part of the community again, like a shepherd that people would follow.

It was great to catch up with what everyone had done in those few months apart. Unfortunately many villagers were still living in the temporary shelters and not much progress had been made. Many houses were still half built. They obviously didn't get any more aid from the leading non-government organisations. Not that we received any cash handouts from the authorities the whole time we were there either, but we had a lot of goods and services provided and some money here and there from private groups. It looked like a lot of that had dried up.

There were all these official ceremonies as part of a national day of mourning, and the Sri Lankan president, President Mahinda Rajapaksa, attended the one in Peraliya along with government ministers and the like; there was a hell of a lot of crying and wailing, which reminded me of the sounds we heard the first day we got to Peraliya. A year on, it came back to everyone and it showed that a lot of the villagers had never got over what happened, and probably never would. The security was pretty tight with a heap of police and army there to ward off a possible opportunistic terrorist attack, I suppose.

The place was certainly greener and a lot of the vegetation had regrown, including mangoes and bananas. The temporary shelters were looking pretty weathered though – some of the roofs had rusted in the sea air – but they were still the only homes many of the people were likely to have for a while, although quite a few new homes had sprouted up. The hardest thing was that too many people were no better off, and some were in fact worse off with all the volunteers, medical help and external food supply gone.

Seeing a young boy called Nuwan broke our hearts. He'd badly burned his legs when he chased a ball while playing cricket and fell into a burning rice pit. He was in hospital for three months. The bandages put on him in hospital had all stuck to his skin and he was in a really bad way, all infected; he was living with his family – his father is blind – in a temporary shelter we'd built with hardly any food and ants all over the place. It was pathetic. Alison went to check on him and left some money for food, but she knew once we left he'd be in a bad way again.

It was good to see Chamilla doing well. She'd set up a pretty well-stocked café in the 100-metre zone selling all sorts of stuff, including warm bottles of Coca-Cola, and I reckon she did a good trade that day with the biggest crowd the village had seen for a long while.

An extraordinary thing Oscar was able to achieve four months earlier was organising a soccer game between the Tamil terrorists and Sinhalese-dominated Sri Lankan army; that's unbelievable. The two groups had been involved in a civil war for over twenty years, although there was supposed to be a truce then, and the traditional resentment for each other was very strong. But Oscar, through an organisation he set up called Football Without Boundaries, was able to get government approval and support plus the backing of the Football Federation, Ministry of Sports, the Sri Lankan army and the LTTE (Liberation Tigers of Tamil Eelam) to make it happen. The game took place at Jaffna, right up the northern end of the country, a city which is very much a Tamil stronghold, deep in their heartland.

The game almost didn't happen, though. A week before it was scheduled to go ahead in August, the ceasefire ended when a sniper assassinated the Sri Lankan Foreign Minister, Lakshman Kadirgamar, in Colombo. That came less than two weeks after the superintendent of police in Jaffna was killed and mutilated after he went to inquire about the death of a Tamil youth in a barber shop, supposedly accidentally shot by a policeman as he put his gun away to get his hair cut. A state of emergency was declared, a curfew issued in Jaffna and the violence pretty much escalated after that. When I heard all that it sort of brought home to me how unstable Sri Lanka can be. The next month a 21-year-old man was playing cricket in Peraliya and a member of a rival tribe from Telwatta, the adjacent village, walked up to him, pulled out a pistol and shot him in the head in cold blood. Nothing was done for fear of further recrimination.

Anyway, incredibly both sides still agreed to use the sporting match as an act of goodwill and peace. It was postponed for a few days but eventually went ahead at the Jaffna army base. The Tamils won 3–0 but players from both sides mixed after the game and the players even hugged after the match. The next day Oscar's team from Galle played the Sri Lankan army and won 5–0; I'm sure Oscar had the competitive juices flowing and was one of the star performers.

Unfortunately a week or two after that Oscar was hit by a bus while riding a motor scooter near Galle. He had his leg in plaster for six or seven weeks; he had broken his ankle pretty badly and had a few gashes that needed stitches too. He's probably lucky to be alive; the only road rule in Sri Lanka is the bigger you are, the more right of way you have – and no one wins when they take on one of those buses!

A lovely Dutch girl, Marjolein Brasl, had also had a motor accident after she went back for a while and she was in even worse condition. Apparently one truck was overtaking another one, both coming in the opposite direction, and forced her motorbike off the road. She broke both her arms, I think, and had to have a bone graft from her hip. She was in Apollo Hospital in Colombo, where I was cared for after I'd collapsed, for quite a few weeks. That was sad news; she is such a wonderful girl, Marjolein.

It was never entirely safe even walking along their roads with the crazy attitude of their drivers. One of the NGO workers, Richie Sixsmith, was also nearly killed while walking home one night when he was hit by a motor cycle carrying a family of four. The father, who was driving, was killed and his wife and children were in a bad way. Richie spent quite some time in Apollo Hospital before being flown back to the UK.

The tsunami warning centre was operating well, the medical centre was still going strong and the school looked like a real school again.

We returned home in late January 2006, and over the next few months I got more and more involved with the MiVAC Trust, which is an initiative of some ex-Australian army engineers and Vietnam veterans who had cleared landmines in Vietnam and had seen first-hand the devastation caused by these indiscriminate weapons. The Trust now includes ex-service personnel from other conflicts, humanitarian aid-workers, members of peace-keeping forces and many concerned civilians. It was started by a Tasmanian, Rob Woolley. The patron is Colonel Sandy MacGregor, one of the most amazing men our country has seen. He was the first soldier to go down the infamous South Vietnamese tunnels during the Vietnam War and received the Military Cross. He was an amazing leader of men who underwent a far greater trauma after the war. In 1987 three of his daughters, along with another teenager, were killed with a shotgun by a paranoid schizophrenic in the other girl's home. Sandy has written several books on self-help and finding purpose in life. He has become devoted to meditation and teaches others, including leading business people, how to handle stress. Incredibly, he decided to meet face to face in jail, and forgive, the man who killed his daughters as a means to helping him move forward in life; can you imagine doing that?

MiVAC has been responsible for some great work in different parts of Asia and the subcontinent. In Cambodia it provided materials for a fence to be built around the perimeter of a school which was bordered by a minefield, thus enabling children to play safely without straying into dangerous areas. Too many had been killed after wandering into minefields. It has also built a waste disposal storage area at the Sunrise Children's Village. MiVAC also funded twelve wheelchairs for Cambodian landmine survivors and other amputees in the Siem Reap Province. It was great to see MiVAC help Sri Lanka, too, by funding – with an equal amount provided by the Royal Commonwealth Society, Tasmania – the rebuilding of an orphanage after a demining project had been completed.

Meanwhile I was definitely a new person with new confidence, new drive, a new set of values and new ambition. As time went on I took on new initiatives and began doing some public speaking about my experiences. To think that that one decision, on Boxing Day 2004, would lead me to having such a life-changing experience, and that I would feature in a documentary movie and then have this book published – well, I'm not sure how many times I have said it in these pages but it's all beyond my wildest dreams. But maybe we don't dream enough about what we can do in life, eh?

12

MOVIE STARS

Sorry for the language, but who would have fucking thought? Poor, plain Donny Paterson looking larger than life on the big screen? Pull the other one, eh? And signing autographs for admiring fans in New York? Wake up, you dreamer. It's bloody well true, though.

On that first day in Colombo when Oscar pulled out the video camera and said he and Alison were going to shoot a lot of our experiences and 'make a film', I thought, 'Sure, they'll send me a copy and I'll sit the family down and watch a home movie in the living room one day.' But due to a correlation of events and the pure power and passion of our story, it grew much, much bigger than that.

I don't know where they got the energy from but after Alison and Oscar returned from their second stint in Peraliya, they embarked on the project of sifting through over 250 hours of film and making a ninety-minute documentary. Through their contacts in the film industry, they were able to get the story of what we had done and some footage to producer Morgan Spurlock, who is best known for the documentaries *Super Size Me* and *Where in the World Is Osama Bin Laden?* Morgan loved what he saw and offered significant editing time and facilities free of charge; he also offered to be executive producer along with Joe Amodei.

You might remember the story about Petra Nemcova, the Czech beauty who was caught in the tsunami while holidaying in Thailand. The model-cum-actress clung to a palm tree, despite a broken pelvis, for eight hours to save her life but, tragically, her fiancé Simon Atlee, a fashion photographer, was washed away to his death. She was to become instrumental in ensuring that the wonderful story of our efforts in Peraliya were portrayed to many people around the world. Alison knew Petra and, obviously being someone who had a special connection with the tsunami victims and the relief work, they hoped she would be someone with 'influence' who might be able to help them. They arranged for a copy to be given to Petra to look at in the hope that she might be impressed by it and open up more doors in the film industry.

The first I knew of anything happening was when Alison contacted me in early 2007 to say the film had been completed and had received rave reviews from those in the industry she had shown it to. She vowed that the film would be released commercially and I'd be going to New York to ride in a stretch limo. Now, I had learned never to doubt what Alison said to me, but this one? 'I'd believe it when I saw it,' I said to myself.

Blow me down, a couple of months later I got an email from Alison saying the documentary was being shown at the famous Tribeca film festival in New York and someone would be sending over some money for me to use for airfares and spending money, and that they'd arranged for me to stay for a week at the Manhattan apartment of a friend who was going to be away, and then with them for a few days. I didn't even know what a film festival was, but I bought myself a decent suit, booked the flight and was off to the Big Apple.

I met up with Alison and Oscar at their apartment where they showed me a promotional poster for the movie. Here I was, like a fucking celebrity actor, at the forefront of this big poster – slouch hat on the bald head and walking stick in hand, in front of the train and rubble from Peraliya. Until then I thought the movie would primarily be about Alison and Oscar and I would play some minor role. Shit, I was on the poster! The poster also had a brilliant 'catch line': 'The first wave brought destruction, the second brought death and then hope arrived – THE THIRD WAVE'.

The screening was scheduled for the next night, 29 April 2007, at the beautiful AMC theatre on 34th Street in New York, and I admit I had no idea what to expect, from the night itself or from the film. It turned out absolutely unreal. Bizarre. I had been asked what my favourite car was and I said a Hummer. Well, can you believe a stretch Hummer swung by to pick us up? It had ten doors and twenty-seven of us got in it – it was just unfuckingbelieeeeevable! There was Bruce, Alison, Oscar, me and other people from our time in Peraliya, plus some I'd never met, all dressed up and going to downtown Manhattan like we were some kind of celebrities. Peraliya volunteers Captain Barry Frishman and his wife, Aleeda, were there; Peter Nossiter and his wife came from England; Stefan, another volunteer who stopped in at Peraliya periodically and entertained the children with a puppet show, came from Germany; and there were others too. All these people had been invited. Alison, Oscar, Bruce and I got the dead-set red carpet treatment, walking down a real carpet strip into the cinema and there were the film promotional posters on the walls on either side of us.

I met Morgan Spurlock at the first viewing and I liked him from the start. He seemed such a down-to-earth, decent bloke who was concerned about humanitarian issues like a lot of us. He was very generous and supportive of the film, providing funds for it to be made so professionally. In 2008 he invited Tracey and me down to Sydney for a special screening of *Where in the World Is Osama Bin Laden?* that he was in Australia promoting. We saw it at the Dendy Cinema at Circular Quay and went for a few drinks and a catch-up afterwards; Morgan signed a promo poster for me, which is a prized possession.

I cried when I watched *The Third Wave* for the first time that night in New York. It was pretty emotional, especially watching myself collapse and be taken to hospital. I cried because of what was being shown, but also because of how proud I felt to be one of four people who were the central figures of a documentary movie. Who in their life gets to be on the big screen in New York City, eh? Not people like me, you'd think. And I was so proud of Oscar and Alison for how good a job they had done. I didn't know Alison had directed a movie before that, called *High Times' Potluck* in 2002, which won an audience award for best feature film at the New York International Independent Film Festival, and best comedy at the Atlantic City Film Festival. Nor did I realise Oscar had produced or co-produced several movies and had been an executive at Stone Canyon Entertainment in Los Angeles.

I was overawed, too, just to be in that world, that environment of celebrity and money. Again, it was another world I never thought Donny Paterson would ever visit. There was a full house to watch the film and the audience gave it a standing ovation at the end before we stood at the front and had a question-and-answer session. People were asking me for my autograph for the first time in my life and some were ripping posters off the wall; they seemed so uplifted by it they wanted a souvenir. Never in my wildest dreams did I think they'd make a movie of our experiences, that the movie would be so successful and, as brief as it was, that I'd be treated like a movie star. It's was surreal.

After one of the showings we went to an 'after party' at the Apple store in Soho, a three-storey building which had a party on each floor. The Tribeca festival was sponsored by Jameson's whiskey and Budweiser beer and plenty of the products were laid on. What a great night; what a great week. The movie was shown at four venues during the festival and received warm reviews and great audience response, with four rousing, prolonged standing ovations.

After the film festival was over Oscar and Alison were great hosts and showed me many of the sights of New York. I made a point of also visiting a New York Knights rugby league team's training session, after making contact with one of the guys on the internet before I left – you've got to keep the flag flying for the sport, eh! The Newcastle Knights gear steward and stadium manager, Neville Allan, was able to provide a set of jerseys to give to them, which was gratefully received. Rugby league is obviously very small-time in the US but they have a healthy little competition going around New York and the north-east corner.

I was fortunate to also be invited down to Chincoteague Island in Virginia by 'Captain Barry', and I was treated to a wonderful few days by him and Aleeda. Barry owns a cruising adventure outfit and he took me out on the water; what a beautiful part of the world it is. Barry was yet another kind-hearted person who took off for Sri Lanka independently to help out, and he proved pretty handy with the hammer and saw during his few weeks there, and we hit it off pretty well – yet another friendship for life to come out of the natural disaster. He has since spent many of the American winters drilling and repairing wells in Third World countries including Liberia, Guatemala and Peru.

Three months later, in June 2007, *The Third Wave* was shown as part of the Sydney Film Festival, and Tracey, the kids and I were invited to attend. Oscar and Alison came out as guests but unfortunately Bruce was busy touring and couldn't make it. It was really special for the film to be shown in our home country and I was so proud and looking forward to being at the screening, and to have my family all there to witness it. But, unbelievably, we couldn't get there because of fierce storms in Newcastle and the Hunter region. Many roads around the area were flooded and we couldn't get to the freeway that links Newcastle with Sydney. The trains were also out of action and we couldn't even get to an airport; we were trapped. At one stage Oscar was talking about hiring a helicopter to get us there but that didn't eventuate. We were so disappointed that we couldn't make it down. Fortunately I was still able to catch up with Oscar and Alison when they came up to our place in Newcastle on their way to far north Queensland. We went with them to see Alison's cousin at Crowdy Head on the New South Wales north coast and had a great few days there with them.

The storms caused an incredible amount of damage in the Hunter and the Central Coast areas north of Sydney, with ten people killed in flash flooding and 4000 people having to be evacuated. We were even affected in our street at Kotara Heights, although our house was fine. Cory and Cooper Vuna, who hadn't been with the Newcastle Knights very long, were outside helping in the neighbourhood; Cooper was getting on with the neighbours like he'd lived there all his life. Karah and Krystal were also getting amongst the mop-up action; a tree went through one lady's house so we invited her to stay with us for a couple of days until the State Emergency Services could come along and remove it and tarp up her roof.

Can you believe that also showing at the Sydney Film Festival at the same time was the doco *Bomb Harvest*, which was created and produced by an old army mate of mine, Laith Stevens. It is about Laos being the most heavily bombed place, per population, in the world and the effect it had on the country during and after the Vietnam War – a subject that became very close to my heart. Laith led a bomb disposal team into Laos and filmed some of his exploits; it's pretty gripping stuff and the movie was nominated for a few awards in Australia. What are the odds that the two of us very ordinary blokes who worked together at the School of Military Engineering in Sydney would one day feature in the same film festival but with different films? Laith still works in the explosive ordnance disposal industry and was working in Kenya recently.

The Third Wave has also been shown at film festivals in Melbourne, Denver, Prague, Toronto, Colorado and Tokyo, the Directors Guild of America festival in Los Angeles, and the Reel Women Film Festival, also in LA, where it won best documentary. Negotiations have been in train for a while now for it to be released worldwide on DVD, including in Australia. It has been taken on by Arts Alliance America and some of the proceeds go to the Happy Hearts Foundation, which was founded by Petra Nemcova.

Back home, I showed the film one night in December 2007 at the Greater Union cinema in Newcastle as a one-off fundraiser for MiVAC, a cause I have become passionate about. Again it received an overwhelming response and the Newcastle Knights players and their coach Brian Smith were really supportive, attending the night and helping with fundraising. People were very responsive; some were quite emotional, gobsmacked really. They knew Donny had gone over there, got a bit crook and come home then went back for a while, but they had no idea what a difference the four of us made. Over three hundred people, mostly friends, family and football connections, attended and we ended up raising $4000 for MiVAC, which funded me going to Laos on a reconnaissance visit to check out some jobs I could do there later. I went over to Laos via Bangkok with a guy called Walter Kopek, who spends half a year in Bangkok and half in the US, and is a devoted worker for MiVAC.

The local newspaper, the *Newcastle Herald*, did a double-page spread leading up to the movie premiere, after having done a few stories on my Sri Lankan adventures previously. At that stage the movie still hadn't been shown extensively in the US or Australia, nor had it been released on DVD. It didn't matter to me; the plight of those affected by the tsunami and the efforts of a special group of volunteers had been shared by probably a couple of thousand extra people from the film festival viewings and our experience had enlightened some people about life elsewhere. To see that given a lasting record by way of a documentary was magic beyond any expectations I had.

Along the way I had a brief moment of fame, and that was just a bonus. It was then back to the regular life for Donald Thomas Paterson. Well, so I thought. The crème de le crème of worldly experiences was about to arrive – in Cannes, during the world's most famous film festival, with some of the world's most famous people, and witnessing opulence I never thought I'd be part of. Bugger me, I still have to pinch myself to remind me that it's not a dream.

13

CANNES AND MONTE CARLO

The first I knew of Sean Penn's involvement in *The Third Wave* was in an email from Alison in March 2008 saying that he saw it, loved it, loved my role and wanted to take it to the Cannes Film Festival. What? You're kidding me! It just so happened that the Academy Award-winning actor (and director) was president of the Cannes Film Festival jury that year, so he arranged to create a first-ever special category, 'the presidential nomination', so that the film could be slotted into the predetermined schedule. Obviously he had some pull. And what's more, he wanted the four of us to go to Cannes for the festival. I'll repeat it again – unfuckingbelieeeeevable!

Alison phoned to advise me that *The Third Wave* was being

shown in Cannes, which meant another trip for me. Initially I thought, 'You beauty! I've never been to far north Queensland before – but surely Alison knows how to pronounce the place correctly?'! She emailed soon after and realised I was not going to Cairns, I was going to bloody CANNES! Next challenge, though, was to pronounce it 'Carne', not 'Cairns', as many people say it.

Naturally I'd heard of the Cannes festival but it wasn't until I did some research on the internet and got to France that I realised how big it is; it's the most famous and prestigious film festival there is, the pinnacle of film festivals worldwide. This time I had no doubts at all that it was going to happen; I still don't know who paid for me to go over and arranged my initial accommodation, but it was all laid on for humble, plain Donny. In May 2008, I flew into Cannes via Paris and had a private car and driver sent to pick me up at the airport and take me to a beautiful flat that had been organised for me a little way out of the main 'strip' along the Mediterranean Ocean. Can you believe it? All I knew was that that night I had to meet Alison and Oscar and the car would be back to pick me up.

I was taken to the InterContinental Hotel but when I reached the revolving front door and was met by the concierge, he wouldn't let me in because I wasn't a guest at the hotel. They required identification as proof that you were a house guest or a guest of a resident, so I had to go to a public phone across the road and call Oscar to come down and verify I was his guest. I didn't know I was going to such a plush place and was only wearing casual slacks and a collared shirt; at least I'd upgraded from my T-shirt and shorts.

Oscar took me into a garden court restaurant and introduced me to Petra Nemcova and Sean Penn. Also there were Bruce; Howard Kiedaisch and Joe Amodei from Arts Alliance America; Morgan Spurlock (who I had met in New York); Morgan's wife, Alexandria; plus a friend of Alison's, Lisa Fox, who is the daughter of Australian transport magnate Lindsay Fox.

It was weird. Obviously I hadn't met Sean or Petra before and had no real perception of what they would be like, whereas they felt they knew me after seeing the film, in which I suppose I exposed myself – my personality, that is – and let out every emotion possible in front of the camera. Sean's greeting was simply, 'Donneeeeee,' then he embraced me and said, 'How are you?' as if he'd known me for years. I'd seen some of his movies but I had no concept of what he might be like as a person. I quickly found out that his welcoming and endearing nature was geniune.

We had a great night, really exciting, as they went through the details of the next evening's red carpet showing and what they thought of the film; they genuinely showed interest in us and not just what we had done in Peraliya. Bruce and I bunked on the floor of Alison and Oscar's suite at the InterContinental that night, the four of us back together just like that first night in Colombo more than four years earlier – this time as close friends for life, not strangers.

The next day we were called up to Sean's penthouse at the InterContinental with its panoramic view over the Mediterranean for a quick chat about something and while we were there he asked where I was staying. I told him I was at an apartment a fair way out of town, and then he asked would I like to stay at his penthouse instead; he had a second bedroom that wasn't being used and it would make it easier for me being much closer to the centre of activity in Cannes. Would I what? He also arranged for me to stay for the duration of the whole festival instead of flying out after three or four days as I'd planned. Sean made a point of saying it was like his haven where he wanted to be able to fly under the radar and kick back, and I had to respect that. He also said there might be a few celebrities coming by and that they would want to be treated the same way, not being bothered by any fanfare, and I should respect their privacy too. I fully understood; there was no way I would abuse that.

Talk about landing on my feet! I looked out at the sea and sort of stopped myself for a minute to take a reality check. Never in my wildest dreams could I have imagined that I would be at the Cannes Film Festival as a character in a movie, let alone sharing a penthouse with Sean Penn, president of the film festival and one of the world's best known actors. But it was fucking real, man, it was happening. And for the rest of the ten days that I was in Cannes, Sean was a wonderful host. Bruce had to fly out the day after the screening to go back on Pearl Jam's world tour but Alison, Oscar and I were included in so many of the social events and went everywhere as part of Sean's private group. I found him such a down-to-earth, considerate guy who is interested in other people and what's around him, not just in himself.

There were a couple of examples that typified this; they may have been little things on his scale but they were big things to me, just like the gesture of the dentist back in Ambalangoda when he treated me for free. The day after I arrived, my tuxedo had gone missing along with my walking stick which I had put on the plane with my luggage. I started to panic a bit and next thing Sean was on the phone arranging with Versace to deliver a suit for the night. As it turned out my tux arrived before our departure so I didn't get to wear the flash one; not that I am complaining – the one I had borrowed from the menswear hire shop in Charlestown, Newcastle, was as good as anything I'd ever worn before. One night a couple of days later I dropped a pair of $15 sunglasses over the balcony (yeah, I'd had a few drinks). Sean heard about that and got me a pair of Versace sunglasses as replacements. That's the sort of guy he is. It mightn't have cost him, I really don't know, but it was just a much appreciated gesture and yet another act he really didn't have to bother himself with. I actually gave the sunnies to Cory as a gift when I got home; he's a celebrity footballer and they probably suit his style more, eh son?

Anyway, when I got back to the InterContinental later that second day, Sean was true to his word; he pointed me to another bedroom at the opposite end of the penthouse to his. He'd actually set it up with some gym equipment but, hey, I could put up with that minor inconvenience! The bed was absofuckinglutely huuuuuge; if I lay across it my feet still wouldn't stick out over the side. And I had my ensuite, all flash marble, all very salubrious. I just chuckle when I think of it – nah, that can't have happened to Donny Paterson. I stayed in these amazing surroundings for ten days at no expense to me. It was … what do they call it? A 'money-can't-buy experience'. And I will be forever appreciative of Sean Penn, who I now regard as a mate.

The next night we were chauffeur-driven to the cinema for the showing of *The Third Wave* and, like in New York, there were promotional posters everywhere and the social photographers all around. This time the poster had an image of Alison, Oscar, Bruce, me and the village chief with a statement from Sean across the top saying: '*The Third Wave* is truly a "must see" – for ourselves, our children and everyone we know; for anyone who has two good legs and a dollar in their pocket. It inspires the very best in us, just when we need that most, and comes as close to answering our purpose in life, more than any other film in my recent memory.' Wow!

Petra walked up the red carpet first and there were flashlights going off everywhere. Obviously no one knew who the four of us 'nobodies' were, so Petra – being the lovely person she is – doubled back and grabbed us to link arms with her and walked back in. It was like a clue to let everyone know we were important, so all of a sudden the cameras were focused on us too.

We were seated near the front and I looked around and there was Bono, the lead singer of the band U2, sitting directly behind me. So, too, was famous documentary maker Michael Moore. There was the celebrated actor Faye Dunaway sitting to my right. Natalie Portman also attended, as well as Morgan Spurlock and other dignitaries.

Sean did a spiel before the movie was screened and introduced us and praised the movie so much. I'll come clean here: I had to hide a tear when I saw it again and got pretty emotional when the whole audience stood and applauded for ages after the screening. As we got to the aisle to walk out, Bono wrapped his arms around me and said, 'That was greeeet, that was greeet,' in his broad Irish accent. To have his approval was just fantastic because he is such a crusader for worthy world aid programs and humanitarian issues. Faye Dunaway asked if I had done any acting and said that I should think about it, that I was a natural – a real-life Indiana Jones. The fourth of the Indiana series was actually shown at Cannes during the festival.

After the screening we were invited to an after-party put on for *The Third Wave* in a marquee on the waterfront. To be honest, I was overwhelmed and felt a little uncomfortable to be wearing a tuxedo and mixing with the VIPs rather than the 'ordinary people' who watched from outside; this was on a much grander scale than Tribeca. But it was another great experience and I took in every moment. After an hour or so we were told 'we're leaving in ten minutes to go on a boat' and I thought, 'That'd be nice, a few of us having a quiet celebration on someone's 18-footer.' So there we were – Alison, Oscar, Bruce and me, plus Bono, Sean and Petra – leaving as a group and heading off in another hire car. Soon after we reached a wharf area that was full of mega yachts and boarded the nicest boat I reckoned I was ever going to have the pleasure of setting foot on. I thought, 'I could kick back here for the night with a few quiet ones, watching the lights of the city over the water.' We were there less than an hour when a 220-seater shuttle vessel came along and transferred the group to an even bigger boat. Stuff me, there I was for the rest of the night, looking at a 92-metre vessel owned by our host, none other than Paul Allen, the co-founder of Microsoft with Bill Gates. When I got home I researched Paul Allen and found out he was worth something like $16 billion, making him the forty-first richest man in the world. He obviously liked his sport

– he owned Seattle Seahawks NFL (American football) and the Portland Trail Blazers NBA (basketball), plus he was part-owner of Seattle's soccer club (the Sounders) to be launched in 2009.

'Donny, mate,' I said to myself, 'you don't mix with *these* sort of people, buddy.' The boat was seven storeys high and had a crew of thirty-five. Paul went around and introduced himself during the night; when we had a brief chat I commented on what an unbelievable boat he had. He told me he had a bigger boat that was in dry dock being painted – it's called the *Octopus* and is 127 metres long!

I can't rattle off all the celebrities who would have been present as I wouldn't have recognised a heap of important people, but Mick Jagger and Kate Hudson were amongst them. That brings me to a funny yet embarrassing moment from the night. I was being introduced to this and that person, mostly from the film industry, and was naturally pretty overawed by the whole affair. I recognised this one dude and after shaking his hand and introducing myself I said, 'Man, do I know you from somewhere? Your face is so familiar.' He just laughed and introduced himself – actor Woody Harrelson. He thought it was funny, actually, but I felt so dumb; but he was really good, just another nice, down-to-earth person who showed an interest in what I was doing there and the film and our work in Sri Lanka. It was a magical night but just one of many in the most amazing week.

The next day we were driven the thirty-seven kilometres to Monaco for the Monaco Film Festival. This time we were given beautiful rooms in the Monte Carlo Casino and it was into the tux again for another celebrity welcome, with Petra adding the glamour (not that you're not glamorous, Alison), and again we were treated like movie stars. There were probably only about fifty people at the Monaco screening but it was nice and intimate. You can usually gauge the audience reaction by the kind of questions asked at the end, and there were plenty of good ones thrown at us. Anyway, the film won the best documentary award, which was a huge buzz, and a great reward for Alison, Oscar, Morgan, Petra, Sean and all those who believed in and backed the movie – and for the people back in Peraliya, too. We went to a function afterwards where I met the actor Tommy Lee Jones, who received an artistic achievement award. Like Cannes, I found Monaco just an incredible playground for the rich and famous.

We then returned to Cannes to enjoy some of the local sights and culture. Sean was busy during the day, of course, in his role as the festival jury president but he would always take the time to have a cigarette, a chat and maybe a drink later in the day. He is a very smart and knowledgeable man. He likes his sport – especially the San Francisco 49ers – and wanted to know about rugby league, Cory's career, my family, what I did back home, world humanitarian affairs and my projects with MiVAC and other initiatives I was trying to set up.

Of a night there was event after event and also my first inside look at how the paparazzi operate. Just to get in the car with Sean with the paparazzi crowded all around was an eye-opener. I never realised how intimidating it is, and how claustrophobic too. One time we got off a boat and a photographer stuck his camera through the open window into the car; some of the paparazzi were so bloody rude, all yelling out his name and trying to get his attention for one cheap snap. Sean was the consummate professional in handling it; it would drive me mad.

All the while Sean had a minder with him, a lovely bloke who looked after the entire group when we went somewhere together. That felt amazing, to have someone watching your back. I imagine people try to get very close to Sean and he could never take his security for granted, especially being so proactive and outspoken on political affairs; you never know what sort of people are out there.

The fame can be beneficial, too, don't worry. I'll never forget one night we went out to a nightclub. It was really crowded and I wondered how we were going to get any space to breathe. Next minute the whole crowd seemed to open up and make way for us as we were led through a door into a private part of the club. All these beautiful girls were serving drinks, as one of the vodka labels was doing a promotion. I was drinking vodka and tomato juice – very high-end! Just being a part of that sort of party, in the entourage of someone famous, was incredible. You couldn't get the smile off my face the whole time.

Another celebrity I met during my stay was Madonna. She popped by to say hello to Sean. I knew they had been married once and it's great to know they'd remained friends. She seemed so unassuming, and I tried to act cool and got her a Coca-Cola and had a chat, all the time dying to ask for her autograph to give to my daughters. I didn't though. Madonna does a lot of work for AIDS in Africa and presented at Cannes a film she wrote, produced and narrated called *I Am Because We Are*, which depicts the plight of women, and the millions of orphaned children caused by the devastation of AIDS in Malawi, from where she adopted a son. I gave her one of my ten copies of *The Third Wave* and she showed a lot of interest in our efforts.

Then there was the night Sean hosted a small party at the penthouse and invited me to stay around. I'll never forget when there was a knock on the door and I got up to answer it. I looked through the peephole and it was Brad Pitt. I thought, 'No way!' We introduced ourselves and had a good chat during the night. He, too, is a real humanitarian who wants to make a difference; he enjoyed watching *The Third Wave*, apparently, after I'd given him a copy. I tried to do my bit as host and served people drinks as an ice-breaker and way of mixing in. Most of the conversation between people was about different world events and humanitarian issues rather than acting; I'd imagine most of those there wanted to leave the 'office' at the office.

A lot of the people were drinking champagne, which I learned cost 450 euros (about A$800) a bottle when I had to ring up room service and order two more. Here I was saying to Sean, 'It'll cost 900 euros for two more, do you think we should order them?' 'Yeah, no worries,' he replied. I did struggle a little bit with the opulence, considering how we got to be there by helping starving, homeless tsunami victims. Going from abject poverty to a penthouse in Cannes, I sure went from one end of the spectrum to the other, but I wasn't complaining. And a good thing was, a lot of those present give lots of money and effort to causes around the world involving the less fortunate.

For me the special thing was that a lot of 'celebs' I met that week spoke to me just like my mates would have done rather than talking down to me, which I appreciated. They were genuinely interested in what Alison, Oscar and I had been doing in Peraliya and how the film came about. That will always be a special memory, and in my eyes Sean Penn will always be a special, genuine bloke who I am very fortunate to know. I also met his wife, Robyn Wright Penn, who is also an actor and who played the role of Jenny alongside Tom Hanks in *Forrest Gump*, among other roles. She is a wonderful person too. She flew in and arrived at the penthouse at about 3 am, and Sean got Alison, Oscar and me out of our beds to drink champagne and have a good chat.

It was funny but when I walked around dressed in a casual shirt and shorts, no one noticed me, but if I walked around with my stick and slouch hat on, many would stop me in the street for a photograph or autograph, obviously having recognised me from the movie poster. That was my bit of fun while I was in Cannes, living up to the image of Donny in the movie, as vain as it seems. With Cory since becoming one of the star footballers in the city of Newcastle, I had just a touch of insight into what he has to get used to around the area; that sort of attention would be a daily occurrence for him. I have always told him to try to give time to the fans, even if it is just a 'G'day, how you going?'. It's important not to forget where you come from. A lot of young footballers get caught up in it; they get good money and lots of press and their heads get too big; the results can be disastrous.

It does seem quite extraordinary that getting such a personal insight into celebrity lifestyles could happen to an ordinary person like me. I've stayed in contact with Sean via email since I returned to Australia. One day, though, I was telling a pain specialist who was treating me about how good Sean had been to me in Cannes and he made a comment that I was just 'a token piece of social conscience'. That affronted me, but when I thought about it, it started to worry me too. I thought maybe that was the case – why would anyone be interested in Donny Paterson? Maybe everyone being nice to me was all just a superficial front while I was at the festival; maybe I was seen as some rough-diamond Aussie ocker who hung around for a few days. Soon after I emailed him about other issues and at the risk of upsetting him, I told him what the doctor had said and asked him straight out: was he genuinely interested in me and my activities? I hoped I wouldn't piss him off by questioning his integrity and genuineness; he might have just told me to piss off, but it nagged at me. Maybe the insecure nature and low self-esteem that I suffered for so long was resurfacing. I won't say what Sean wrote back, that's personal between us, but he certainly reassured me that the doctor was out of line, and wrong, and shouldn't have commented about something or someone he knew nothing about.

Sean has certainly proved it since by staying in touch. And when Cory went over in 2008 to trial as a gridiron 'punter' with a few of the NFL franchises, including Sean's beloved 49ers, Sean and Robyn made a special effort to meet up with him at a bar and spend a couple of hours chatting to him. That says something, eh? That was just about the highlight of Cory's visit, and it was special for me, too, to be able to do something out of the ordinary for him after some tough times I'd put him through when he was younger.

14

PERALIYA AND ITS PEOPLE TODAY

I desperately wanted to return to Peraliya – at least by the fifth anniversary of the tsunami in December 2009 – to see for myself what had happened to the village and to find a bit of 'closure' on that incredible part of my life. The end of the Tamil war in May 2009 was the prompt for me to hop on a plane and do it; I felt I could do something for those so badly affected by the war.

The Tamil war ended after the LTTE surrendered, having been pushed back to a small area in the far north of the country, surrounded by 50,000 Sri Lankan troops. After twenty-six years

PERALIYA AND ITS PEOPLE TODAY

the Tamils gave up their claims, but who knows if minority groups will rise again.

I wanted to replicate to a degree what we had done in 2005 and help the refugees who had been held captive by the LTTE soldiers. But when I arrived I was advised by all my contacts there that there was no chance I would be allowed into the IDP (Internally Displaced People) camps around Vavuniya, so to that extent it was a bit of a wasted exercise. Maybe I was being a bit naive; this time it was a military issue not a natural disaster and the Sri Lankan army was providing little access to outsiders, even NGOs and the UN.

But the trip (I was there for eighteen days) certainly wasn't in vain for me because I was able to visit Peraliya and see how life there was four and a half years after the tsunami. It was an emotional experience to go back there and, even though the once-devastated part of the coastline had new buildings and new life in it, it reacquainted me with the tough, poor, volatile place that is Sri Lanka today.

And events I'd been informed of in the intervening years had already proved that to me. In 2007 Kumara was butchered in an inter-village or gang-related slaying. It had something to do with an argument over one of the shelters he was living in. Apparently he was attacked by a gang and chopped to pieces with a machete – it sent shivers down my spine thinking of it. Poor Kumara just had no peace after the tsunami hit and was a really troubled soul, but no one deserved a death like that. I still have the portrait of his family with their faces superimposed over the top of my family's, and I think of him often.

Mr Fernandopulle was assassinated in April 2008, joining a long list of government officials and even journalists who had met their deaths at the hands of terrorists. He was about to officially start a marathon race, which was part of the Sinhala and Tamil New Year celebration in Weliveriya, when a suicide bomber ran through the crowd and exploded himself. It was all caught by television cameras and you can watch it on YouTube, which I don't find a good thing. Fourteen people were killed including Mr Fernandopulle, who was waving a flag to start the race. Also killed were Sri Lanka's national athletics coach, Lakshman de Alwis, and Olympic marathon runner KA Karunaratne. More than sixty people were injured. It's just so, so sad that those sorts of things go on so regularly in Sri Lanka.

Peraliya was confronted, in a pretty big way, with the war of independence staged by the Tamil Tigers when, in January 2007, a suicide bomber killed herself and eight passengers, and wounded fifty other people, when she blew up a bus as it stopped along the Galle Road in the village. Only a day earlier six civilians had been killed in another bus blast just north of Colombo. It is just bloody sad to think that around 70,000 people have been killed in this fighting over a quarter of a century and innocent people have lived in so much terror. Many people hardly have enough money to feed and clothe themselves and have to endure terrible medical facilities, but they will arm themselves with automatic weapons and ammunition.

I felt anxious during the plane trip and was so looking forward to seeing Chinthu and Dinesh particularly. But first I had arranged to meet Greg Evans, one of the volunteers from America who had returned to live at a place called Negombo near Colombo. With the assistance of Greg and his contacts I hoped to get an indication of whether I could get into the refugee camps in the north of the country and help the people who had reportedly been living in terrible conditions. But that was not to be.

My first impression when I touched down in Colombo was how oppressive it was; the heat and humidity was stifling and the air was thick with pollution as well, making breathing difficult. It took me a few days to get used to it again.

When I met up with Greg that first day I skolled down a Lion lager faster than I'd ever drunk a big bottle of beer, thanks to the combination of the flight, the heat and emotion of being back in Sri Lanka and seeing Greg again. Greg had been able to get a five-year visa to return to Sri Lanka and had set up a business selling meat products to restaurants. He'd teamed up with a local chef who cooks the meat which is then snap frozen ready for distribution to restaurants.

After three days in Negombo I left for Colombo and stayed with Ravin, a Sri Lankan who I'd also kept in contact with since he was in Peraliya helping the Israeli aid team. I was on a mission to find Toyna, our driver from the first trip, and ask him to take me down to Peraliya. Ravin and I went to the district where I knew Toyna lived and asked around about him; we had a photograph of him that we hoped someone would recognise but were getting no responses. I was becoming frustrated and about to give up when I decided to give it one more go in the next street. If we had no luck we'd call it quits. Ravin approached a man and asked him if he knew Toyna and he nodded his head. He couldn't tell us where he lived but whistled someone else over who knew his house and could explain how to get there. We'd been within a few hundred metres of Toyna's home. I can't explain the jubilation and the relief I felt.

We reached Toyna's home and I called out, 'Toyna ... Toyna are you home? It's me Donny!' A man I didn't recognise opened the door and I froze. 'Toyna must have moved,' I thought. It turned out that the man was a visitor, and when Toyna eventually came down the flight of stairs, his jaw dropped; he looked in total disbelief at seeing me after four years. We embraced and it was like being reunited with my family; our bond is that close.

Next day Toyna and I made the trip down the coastline to Hikkaduwa. All along the road I could see new houses, and the landscape was nothing like when I last travelled that route. The trees and palms had grown; people were busy getting about their lives rather than standing around, and all seemed to have returned to how it must have been before the tsunami. The trip, which had taken four to five hours before, this time took just over two on the rebuilt road. Toyna smiled and explained in his broken English that the president lived down this way. Yet one thing that hit me while covering those miles was how many young men on the streets, many of them kids really, were armed with large guns.

When we arrived at Hikkaduwa we pulled up at the guesthouse where I had stayed previously. The people there were happy to see me, but I felt their rooms were overpriced and stayed only one night. I decided to head back to my original 'home', Casa Lanka, where we had stayed the first few weeks back in 2004, even though it was much more basic. The owners, a lovely couple, were very welcoming and I was happy to give them some income, as they were still struggling. I then set about locating the tuk-tuk driver I had used before, only to find he'd been quite ill with gall bladder problems and his son, Pradeep, was running the tuk-tuk. The mother, father and son turned up next day and it was great to see them; they had lived in terrible conditions in their little shop after the tsunami. After hearing about how expensive their medical bills were, I was happy to use Pradeep whenever I needed a ride somewhere.

When I returned to Peraliya it was as if it was a new town on the old site. I saw few familiar faces; as so many people, fearing another tsunami, had left the village for 'safer' areas inland or more sheltered places further down the coast towards Galle. The landscape was thicker with jungle growth and there was an abundance of new homes, many of them quite comfortable.

Probably about fifty of the hundreds of temporary shelters we had erected remained but no one was living in any of them. Most were overgrown by vegetation and just waiting to fall down, while others were being used as storage sheds behind permanent dwellings. Strangely, Kumara's house and his temporary shelter stood there unoccupied – eerie, considering the circumstances of his death. I saw Kumara's father working with some people making rope out of coconut husks. He looked sober and healthy and he remembered me; the first thing he said, after calling me 'machan' (which means 'friend') was, 'Kumara dead'. How do you recover from such misery; seeing your son lose his wife and children and then him being butchered to death?

The school, which now has 400 students, was magnificent. It had buildings four storeys high, arranged in a big square with the only remaining buildings from 2005 being the two-storey school block and the library. The school is now surrounded by a big fence with double gates as an entry. Obviously a lot of funding had been provided from overseas and from the Sri Lankan government. It was just fantastic to see kids running around and being happy like in a school yard anywhere; I didn't recognise any of them – most would have looked very different four years ago and obviously a lot of the children I knew had left the village.

My visit to the school was a real highlight of my trip. The headmaster recognised me immediately; he came to me and said, 'Hello Mr Donny,' as if he'd known me all my life and gave me a vigorous handshake and a magnificent head wobble. He explained how the Italians had come through with their promise and rebuilt the place. He took me to the IT room where there were twenty-seven computers. After visiting other areas of the school he took me to the library. As he opened the door and went inside then motioned me to come in, I couldn't move. It just struck me that I was back at 'the heart' where each day had begun for us. I eventually managed to walk inside and it was truly amazing. It was like I went into a trance with my mind racing back to the faces and the conversations that had filled that room – a hub of desperate activity – while now it was a place of such quiet and peace. I was so pleased that the children had such a facility, a far better one than they had had before the tsunami, and I was glad I had the opportunity to catch up with the headmaster, who is a wonderful man.

The medical centre in the village takes pride of place and would be the best equipped centre outside of a major city in Sri Lanka. It doesn't just offer medical services but also health education to people in the region to help improve their standard of living. It was very much the brainchild of Dr Thomas Stein from Hamburg, who continues to visit and work there, as do some other overseas doctors. The building was designed by an Australian architect, Justin Hill.

As was the case on my previous visits, other Sri Lankan villages have continued to express resentment that Peraliya has received so much government and international attention, and claim that many other areas of the coastline are being neglected in favour of the area around the train wreck. And a lot of conflict still exists in Peraliya itself, with people jealous if others have more than them. I heard reports of some families who pre-tsunami had an extended family all crammed into one house but who now have two houses, so some people are better off than before the tsunami.

Most people want a second storey on their newly built homes so that they will be well off the ground if a tsunami hits again, but what you see is a lot of homes with strongly built brick bottom storeys but the top levels remain unfinished because the money ran out. The chief was accused of spending aid money on his own house but I know that is not the case; he used his own money or private donations given directly to him.

PERALIYA AND ITS PEOPLE TODAY

I spent a little time with the chief and he filled me in on events. He had retired from work and his sons ran his fishing business where he had four boats. He is still very much the leader of the village and says that within three years he would like to sell his house in Peraliya and convert it into an elders' retirement home. He asked for assistance in having a fence built around the temple, which is such a monument in their culture; he says people had too much access to it and too often left it and its surrounds untidy.

Still, I didn't see anyone hanging around looking for handouts in Peraliya. People were back to their normal lives and jobs and things seemed quite prosperous by their standards. A lot of people were back out working on boats, with fishing obviously again the main source of income. It appears some fishermen received three or four boats from funding while others had been given no assistance. Two new boat factories have been built along the coast. There has also been a mask shop set up in the village, a mixed-produce store, two brick stores and other small businesses, which have helped diversify the village from being almost purely dependent on fishing.

I had a very emotional reunion with Chinthu, who I'd kept in regular contact with via email messages over the years; many of his giving me an insight into how ghastly his life was in the front line of the war. He looked like a changed man; like he'd seen too much war. He also seemed more aloof, and there was distance in his eyes. Although he looked every bit as fit as when I'd last seen him, he seemed physically exhausted and emotionally drained. But it was so good to be together again and we caught up with each other's lives in more detail than our emails allowed. He was back on the roster of forty-five days of work in the army then ten days leave.

During out couple of days together he gave me more first-hand accounts of his experience as a front-line platoon commander (rank of lieutenant). I could hear in his voice how proud he was of his men and his army. He said with real passion, 'I love Sri Lanka, I love the president and I love the army.' But he displayed the scars of someone who is young but has seen so much suffering and death. He explained how thirty-eight members of his battalion had been killed in action and some forty others injured. Before he left to go back on duty the monks held a ceremony to bless him. It was a privilege to witness it; and a relief to know that he did not have to return to active service.

Not only did Chinthu have the war to contend with he'd been ripped off by a carpenter who was building his house, an episode which is typical of the tales of corruption you hear too often over there. Chinthu had given the bloke quite a bit of money to finish off the construction of his house but he disappeared with the money, leaving the top storey hardly begun.

PERALIYA AND ITS PEOPLE TODAY

As a result, Chinthu had to mortgage his house and rent it out for a while as he lived at his parents' place. He still didn't have a proper roof on his home, so the water ran down inside the walls when it rained and caused a bad rising-damp problem. At least he still had his wife and daughter, and he had hope, but you could see the stress on his face.

I spent the most time with Dinesh, still a wonderful young man, who took me along the coast sightseeing for a few days. He'd sold his electrical business but was subcontracting to the man who bought it. One thing that shocked me was when he revealed how Kumara had intimidated and threatened him while I was there (particularly during the time I returned to Australia when I was ill), and how people of the village had threatened to kill him because they thought he was being given handouts from me during the times we were rebuilding Peraliya. He told me about the time Kumara put a gun to his head and pulled the trigger (it obviously didn't go off) and said, 'Next time it will go bang.' Kumara told him, 'Just leave and disappear; I don't want to see you around Donny.' I used to think he and Kumara were tight; I was stunned.

My time with Dinesh, too, was emotional, but it was also a great relief for both of us to see each other in the flesh again. We had a lot of fun too; I don't think he'd laughed as much in a long time; and neither had I.

I also met up with our interpreter Chamilla and her husband and daughter, and they took me up to Alluthawalla, which I last saw as a terrible refugee camp. It had been relocated from that jungle camp to a purpose-built village with over sixty houses, a playground and public wells. The wonderful Texan Larry Buck and his organisation Bread for a Hungry World had provided a lot of aid to relocate the Alluthawalla village and people, who were very happy in the new environs.

Chamilla and her family live on a block of land in a beautiful house which the Irishman Jeff gave a lot of assistance to build. Chamilla's husband, who was home only briefly, returned to Libya where he works driving trucks. Their little daughter, who had grown up into a beautiful girl with impeccable English, goes to the International School of Galle. Chamilla's lovely little café within the 100-metre zone had been closed down. There was no one living in that zone around Peraliya or Hikkaduwa, although there were in areas closer to Colombo. I was left wondering how far the 'no building within 100 metres of the shore' edict reached up the coast.

One thing that remains near the shoreline is a beautiful monument to those who died. The memorial reads: 'The president of the Socialist Republic of Sri Lanka on this day 26th of January 2006 in memory of 1270 train passengers [most estimates of the death toll are closer to 1700, and I have used the most quoted figure of 1643] and 249 villagers who lost their lives due to the tsunami on 24-12-2004 at Peraliya'. Built into the stone are images of people being swept away by the water; the train and cars from the road dominate. In addition a 16-metre-high statue of Buddha has been erected, with the names of thousands who perished in the region listed underneath it.

Two of the most damaged carriages from the *Queen of the Sea* stood at the railway station at Hikkaduwa for some time, while the people at Peraliya campaigned for them to be on display there as that was the true site of its disaster. As it turned out, they were removed completely as they had started to rust and attracted beggars trying to get money from tourists; even children were skipping school to beg for money there. The rest of the train was brought back into service between Colombo and Galle. It actually returned to Peraliya on Boxing Day 2008 for the tsunami's fourth anniversary, when a religious ceremony and memorial service was held.

One of the volunteers organised a photographic museum of the tsunami and mop-up, which is a very powerful testament, and it features some of Buddhika's drawings. I couldn't find out what he was up to – he'd be nearly nineteen now – but I hope he is progressing with his incredible artistic talents.

It was a strange feeling to spend a few days in Peraliya. I felt so happy that the people had their homes and their lives back.

But in another sense I felt disconnected from the village. I came across probably only a dozen people I knew from my time there, and although they embraced me on my return and were happy to see me, it just seemed a different place to the one that had had such an impact on my life.

I was frustrated in a sense, too, that some of the permanent buildings we had busted our guts to build were rotting away – one reason being that some of the people we had built them for had another house or two somewhere else. I felt a bit cheated by people's deceit but, as I have stated, people in desperate times do desperate things. But the deepest impression I was left with was that people had moved on, either geographically or in the way they lived their lives, and I didn't need to worry any more. Their lives had been restored.

Nevertheless, on the train trip back to Colombo I received another chilling insight into their civil war. Sitting next to us was a young man who I found out was twenty-two, the same age as my son, Cory. He was obviously in some pain and had his forearm bandaged. With Dinesh as interpreter, he told me about how he had been involved in a battle during which he was shot in the thigh. He continued to fight until he was shot in the forearm and then had to lay down his weapon because he simply couldn't fight any more. Once the army won the battle, they moved forward and came across the bodies of their combatants … they

PERALIYA AND ITS PEOPLE TODAY

were all women! The young soldier showed us a video of the gunfire and the bodies after it ended, which he had taken on his mobile phone after he was injured. I choked up and wondered what sort of psychological scars he would carry from ordeals like these … and how I would feel if had to greet my son getting off a train with this man's injuries, physical and mental, after returning from the war zone.

Going back to Peraliya provided some closure for me. I left this time being able to say it was a past chapter in my life and I, too, could move on. I was satisfied our group of volunteers had done something that has had a happy, long-term effect, but I've also lost a link with the people, the place and the event I was part of; so there was a bit of grieving as well. Maybe it's time to put my energies into other areas of the developing world that might need assistance.

And the other volunteers today?

I keep in contact with many people from our time in Peraliya and I have caught up with quite a few when they have come to Australia or when I was in the US; we all know there is always an open house and a spare bed whenever we are close geographically. Many people's lives were changed by our experiences in Sri Lanka and many of us are still trying to make a difference to the lives of those less fortunate. That's magic.

Bruce, who was in Sri Lanka in 2009, has kept up his support of the people in Peraliya and nearby villages with several self-sustaining projects, spending thousands of his own dollars. His newest venture is a coconut oil mill at Welamudda that employs sixty people. Three brick machines are still operating and earning an income for quite a few people, and a sawmill still operates there. Bruce has organised a spice mill and hopes to be exporting spices by the end of the year. He is also working on a solar-powered ice-making machine for them as well, so that they have alternative industries. A home for elders has been completed and nine elderly women live there.

In between all his ongoing efforts, Bruce has been working as a chef on a ranch in Colorado, skiing the back country peaks when he can and touring with some leading bands. He is hoping to be in Australia with Pearl Jam in November 2009 and I very much look forward to catching up with my good buddy, one of the world's great people.

Alison has also kept in regular contact with people in Sri Lanka, and her efforts to help there have continued beyond funding the tsunami early-warning station. On my return visit I found out some of the personal things Alison has done for the people there since she returned to the US – like paying for Chamilla's daughter to attend the International School and helping some other families in a small way, with limited donations from others. She still wants to go back and possibly work in displacement camps and help once the political landscape has settled a bit. I'd love to join her if that could be organised.

Alison and Oscar are producing another documentary film on the Dirty Hands Caravan initiative of Sean Penn, which should be very good. It is about four buses Sean organised to take young volunteers across the US, as they carried out community projects along the way – like cleaning parks and neighbourhoods and caring for the sick and needy. It's typical of Sean's community and humanitarian instincts to do such a thing.

Sean was one of many who appeared at the Coachella Valley Music and Arts Festival, in April–May 2008. The 'caravan' left southern California, where the festival was held, and took off for New Orleans. About 150 people who attended the festival hopped on the buses and about that many again joined for varying periods along the route. They did some amazing things like cleaning up and repairing the homes of poor people, building houses or shelters for the homeless, protesting the Iraq war while supporting the needs of veterans and their families, planting native trees, cleaning up parks and wetlands, and pretty much helping people in need. Sean only organised it over the few weeks preceding the festival, so it just shows what people with the right intentions can do in their own communities. I can't wait to see the film.

Oscar and Alison have continued to work on the promotion of *The Third Wave* and to have it released to the mass market on DVD; it continues to have special viewings at film festivals. As I write this, *The Third Wave* had just been shown at the City of Angels Film Festival on Sunset Boulevard in Los Angeles and won the 'most inspiring' documentary award. The big news is that it hit cinemas in the US this year – what a buzz and what a reward for Oscar and Alison and all those who backed and believed in the movie.

Sebastian left the medical profession, believing he could do more to bring attention to the plight of people who have suffered so much in natural disasters by producing documentaries, and he was back in Sri Lanka in 2009, working on a film with Greg assisting him; I'm not sure what the subject was exactly.

15

DONNY TODAY

I love Tracey and my three children to death. It's sad that I wasn't able to show it well enough through too many dark years (and probably still don't) but I'd like to think I have a great relationship with them now. A father couldn't hope to have better kids than what we have, and Tracey should take a lot of credit for that. Forgiving oneself is part of the twelve-step program that I learned way back during one of my attempts at rehabilitation, and that was what I had to do. We've got a granddaughter now – Karah's daughter, Tayah-Lili – and we have many more years to grow as a family.

My main mission now is developing an organisation I have created called Brick-Aid, which basically involves having in place an international hit-team that can go to Third World countries affected by disaster – flood, famine or earthquake – and provide immediate, expert, on-the-ground support. My experiences in Peraliya and other projects I have since done in Laos have equipped me for that. We named the organisation Brick-Aid because I believe it's about rebuilding lives a brick at a time. I want to set up a small potent team of five or six people – doctor, paramedic, water supply expert, logistics expert, someone who can look at finance and budgeting, and me. The mission would be to head to the affected place and start making a difference from the ground with independent decision-making and not be subject to the red tape and bureaucracy that the bigger organisations suffer from, as we found first-hand in Sri Lanka. Donations to Brick-Aid helped fund my trip to Sri Lanka in June 2009.

I am still involved with MiVAC and remain passionate about it. I went to Laos in 2008 and built a toilet block and water well for the 500 or so people in the village of Teme Po Poon, all financed by MiVAC. It made a big difference to their standard of living. The interesting thing was, we had to show the villagers how to use the toilets we installed, and how to keep them clean – it was bucket flush. A lot of them had never seen a toilet before.

Children had to walk six kilometres one way just to get water and then cart it back, which was a day's tough toil for them, while the adults worked in the fields. That means the children would miss a day's school, and they had to transport the water at least a couple of days a week. We had to dig to forty metres to find water and it took several drills but suddenly all of them had water any time of day. It changed the whole village plus enabled the kids to go to school when they should have. They are a fairly nomadic race, moving every few years, but now that they have permanent water they will hopefully stay in the location a lot longer.

They are very poor people who farm rice and bananas in an attempt to be self-sufficient but so much of the land in Laos is not arable; yet they would give you their last grain of rice. People in the village thought we were heroes for providing them with a source of fresh water – it changed the lives of everyone in the village. We also took soccer balls with us and gave them to the children; some had never seen a ball before, and it was great to see the faces of young children who had so little light up again, just like back in Sri Lanka.

The danger with these nomadic tribes is that when they move around and clear land to farm, they too often hit unexploded bombs and landmines. MiVAC come in and contract companies to clear a place first then put schools up and build a well and ensure there is safe ground for farming. Fortunately the people are becoming less nomadic now and are learning to use the earth for longer periods of time.

The situation in Laos is just tragic. I don't think any Asian country suffered as much due to war last century. The North Vietnamese invaded Laos and occupied the eastern parts, which led to the Americans launching regular bombing raids on the Vietcong-occupied territories; then the South Vietnamese invaded certain regions. One report I read said that the massive American aerial bombardment saw Laos hit by an average of one B-52 bomb-load every eight minutes, twenty-four hours a day, between 1964 and 1973. To think that thousands of people are still regularly affected by unexploded bombs more than thirty years since the end of the Vietnam War and the Laos civil war is just mind-boggling. But it's no wonder; the Americans have a lot to answer for.

The 'cluster bombs' have left the worst legacy. They are small explosive 'bomblets', many of which look just like small balls, which were dropped by air or launched by rocket in large canisters containing hundreds of the 'bombies'. The canisters would open in mid-air, scattering the bomblets over a wide area. Each bomblet contained 300 metal fragments, and if they all detonated, about 200,000 steel fragments would be propelled over an area the size of several football fields, creating a deadly killing zone. They could do terrible things to soft tissue and organs: a single fragment could rupture the spleen, or cause the intestines to explode – and that's what the bombs were designed to do.

Unbelievably, something like ninety million CBU-bomblets, just one of twelve kinds of cluster bomb, were dropped on Laos. Can you credit that?

About a quarter did not detonate and are still sitting there, virtually becoming landmines. Children often find them and are attracted to their bright colours and either the ball shape or butterfly-like shape; they think they are toys and throw them around and play with them. When moved they explode, and I saw so many children and adults during my visit who were without limbs; it was just shocking.

While in Laos I went to the town of Savannakhet, and met officials from several non-government organisations during my four-week trip. I also met with a Japanese organisation called SVA (Shanti Volunteer Association) which does a lot of work in Laos. I must admit I looked pretty poorly on the Japanese race after what they did to our soldiers during World War II and how they ignore the world's overwhelming sentiment against their blatant and unnecessary hunting and butchering of whales. But I was left with great admiration for what they were doing in Laos. They mainly build schools, wells and toilets.

We also travelled to schools MiVAC had helped build and met the Minister for Education. We found other towns and villages that needed help and we're trying to raise more money to get back and assist where we can. There is so much work that needs to be done over there, not just with the landmine problem and mine ordnance, but with their infrastructure. It's a very poor country. At least in Sri Lanka they have the ocean and can fish, they have that extra food source if the land is not kind to them. If the crop doesn't grow in Laos, they starve.

Another initiative I have become involved with is helping street kids in Newcastle through the Awabakal Aboriginal Co-Operative based at Wickham. Basically it provides a bus service on Friday and Saturday nights from 9 pm to 2 am to get the youth off the street. Often kids fear going home because Mum or Dad are too pissed or too stoned, or there are other domestic issues that force the kids to feel they have to be out of the house. Ultimately they wander the streets in boredom and frustration and in many cases get themselves into trouble. The more we get them off the streets and counsel them, then take them home, the less likely they are to get into trouble.

Unfortunately I haven't been able to help for a few months since my knee replacement in October 2008 but I will again soon. I used to go out on 'patrol' about once a month and we usually team up as a male and female partnership, so that we can identify with both sexes. With my background – a teenager with a far from happy home life at times, and my addictions as a parent – it is easy for me to get on their level and understand their issues. It is sad to hear 'I don't really want to go home' because of drug-taking or drunkenness or sexual assault.

I'm still involved with the Newcastle Wests junior players, and I am hoping to do some youth development work with the Newcastle Knights in the future. I get such a kick out of seeing young players develop as footballers and as people. In 2009 I was also appointed as trainer to the combined Affiliated States team for the under 18s Australian Secondary Schools National Championships in Newcastle. I also enjoy helping out the indigenous side of rugby league and go away with the Newcastle team as a sports trainer for the annual Aboriginal Rugby League knockout, which is played at different venues throughout New South Wales, like Redfern Oval in Sydney, or in Kempsey or Armidale.

I'd never been a public speaker before although I've always felt confident enough doing presentations or speaking in front of groups. Alison Thompson's parents are heavily involved in the Rotary Club at Cronulla in Sydney, which funded computers at the early-warning centre at Peraliya and helped with other schemes while we were there. Anyway, they asked me down a couple of times to do talks and they seemed to go okay.

Word of my experiences got around Newcastle a bit and in 2007 the Newcastle Knights asked me to speak to their talented young players at their annual presentation function (in a question/answer interview format), basically to talk about what happened in Sri Lanka and the success of the film. The message I try to convey is just what can happen if you go for it and believe in yourself. That led to me being asked to be keynote speaker at the Excalibur Club, which is a corporate supporter club for the Knights, and I've addressed a few Lions Clubs as well, and the Sri Lankan community at Castle Hill, who raised some money to assist with rebuilding projects in Sri Lanka. Even Krystal's school has had me up a couple of times to talk to the students, which I find very rewarding; the school donated money to Brick-Aid, which was tremendous.

Generally I have more energy day to day, and a greater desire to do things with my time, and I feel a lot more content within myself. I don't battle with the 'what ifs' of my army days anymore. All those years Tracey would tell me I was a good person but she couldn't get through no matter how hard she tried. The Queen of England could have told me that I was a good person and I wouldn't have believed her; I was taking medication but just couldn't shake the depression.

In Perth we had our own house and I loved getting into the yard and garden. We've rented for a long while now but one of our ambitions for 2009 is to get our own house in Newcastle, which we have decided we will call home no matter what happens in Cory's football career and where he ends up playing.

One of our great joys as a family is to have seen Cory become an established first grade player in the best rugby league competition in the world, the National Rugby League here in Australia. There is no greater feeling as a parent than to see your son or daughter achieve what he or she set out to do. Cory followed his dream by coming to Newcastle from Perth at the age of sixteen and all his hard work, together with the encouragement and good coaching he has received, has paid off.

In 2006 he was chosen to play in the Junior Kangaroos side, which is the Australian under-19 team from which so many players go on to become full international representatives. The next year he made his first grade debut for the Knights and in 2008 he was chosen in the Prime Minister's XIII to play against Papua New Guinea in Port Moresby. The PM's team is seen as a side of the 'next generation' of Test or State of Origin players, an encouragement squad of rising stars, most of whom are at a level just below major representative honours. I have no doubt Cory will play for New South Wales in State of Origin, or for Australia, if he stays injury free. When he does I will be so proud of him.

I try to know my place when it comes to Cory's footy. I'm not living my unfulfilled dreams through my son; I was never going to have a sporting career. We always go and watch his games as a family. There are times when I see him get hurt and the subject of a big hit, and I get very nervous before a match. I liken rugby league to sending your son off to war; we're sending them into battle, they are modern-day gladiators to me. They go out and physically bash each other non-stop for eighty minutes. When I see Cory do some highly skilled thing on the ground and people call out his name, it's just so rewarding knowing where he came from as a footballer when he was five years old, and I had been there watching that development all the way. I can't believe how drained footballers are after a match; the physicality is extraordinary; injury is the biggest fear of a player or parent. Americans who have watched matches can't believe the impact of the tackles and that our players don't wear padding or helmets.

We're still not as close as I'd like it to be – Cory left home when he bought his own place and moved in with his girlfriend – but I am doing everything in my power to have a relationship far better than I had with my father. Cory's much closer to his mother, very close in fact, but … one brick at a time, eh? Cory leads a very busy life, too, but he knows I support him fully. When we do get together it's good, and I really look forward to going into the dressing room after the Knights games and seeing Cory and some of the boys that I've got to know well.

There was a bit of publicity around Cory when he was invited to trial as a punter with some NFL clubs in the US in late 2008, just a couple of months before former Australian football player Ben Graham went to the Super Bowl with the Arizona

Cardinals. Oz Punt, an organisation of talent scouts who look at prospective NFL players in Australia, arranged the trip for him. It's ironic that he no longer does a lot of goalkicking with the Knights, although he is the understudy goalkicker to Kurt Gidley and does the kick-offs and 'punts' the ball in open play occasionally. He can certainly whack a ball a long way with his right boot – down the field and upwards into the air, which is important with 'hang time' so valuable in the NFL.

Cory spent some time with the American national kicking coach who was impressed with him and gave him some pointers; the ball is a lot narrower in American football, of course. Cory couldn't believe the equipment, the set-up, the detail of their preparation; he said they had a coach for everything and reckons they'll have a coach for the water boys soon. He toured some stadiums and went to a couple of games and was invited into dressing rooms afterwards – what a great experience for him. And to meet Sean and Robyn Penn while he was there – not a bad experience for a 21-year-old ex-army brat (as soldiers regularly refer to their children). The Arizona Cardinals said he could return any time he liked and they'd consider a contract but he feels he has a lot to achieve in rugby league first, and if he was to entertain a move to the States he could do it at any age.

Karah has taken very well to the challenge of being a young mother to Tayah-Lili, with the support of our family, and she is growing as a young woman and a mother. She is the greatest. She is a qualified beauty therapist but has chosen to change her career by doing a security guard course and she works one or two nights a week at some of the hotels and nightclubs around Newcastle. Karah enjoys playing rugby union with the local Merewether club (there is no women's rugby league in Newcastle).

Krystal is in Year 11 at high school and has a bubbly, vivacious personality and loves socialising with her friends; she recently obtained her driver's licence so she's not home too often these days. She has played basketball and touch football but she chooses not to get too serious about any sport, instead just making herself available to play when needed. She has done a little modelling and applied to be the face of Privvy, a ladies' fashion shop, and made it to the finals. She also did a catwalk for them and a photo shoot; she enjoyed it and it gave her a good sense of what a model's life would be like. Krystal has done some hair modelling too, for a competition that Wella was running, which gave her exposure in all the Price Attack catalogues. She is on the modelling books of an agency in Newcastle called Models and Actors, so who knows – she might get to Europe one day as a fashion model.

Tracey, other than organising me, works for Allambi Youth Services, which is a service that takes care of the needs of out-of-home children and young people with high needs, including those with disabilities. In February 2009 she was given the opportunity to move across to the foster care team and now works in foster care training and recruitment, which provides assessment and training of potential foster carers. Caring for others, eh? She's had plenty of practice there with old Donny as a husband! I can't begin to thank her and vow my undying love for her; she has been my saviour on more than one occasion and has been a wonderful woman, wife and fantastic mother. I truly was blessed the day Tracey came into my life.

We don't talk about my dark times much, the kids and I. They have accepted that that was what Dad was like at that period of time, and know that I have grown and beaten the odds. I think they admire me for that more than disliking me for what I put them through.

I've had no problems with morphine or pethidine for over ten years now, with the use of prescribed non-addictive pain relief enabling me to get through. I've been clean since 1997 and doctor shopping doesn't exist in my life anymore. Late in 2008 I had to have a replacement of my right knee joint which meant a lot of pain and the need for painkillers. Because I have such a tolerance to the drugs it was always going to be a difficult experience for me and I fully explained my dilemma to the surgeon. I am very grateful for how I was treated. The medical staff knew of my tolerance and past abuse and they were able to take that into consideration and give me the large amount that I needed, but controlled it and monitored me closely and treated me humanely. I have a bizarre record at the Mater Hospital in Sydney for the greatest amount of morphine administered post-operatively to any patient on record. It's a dubious record to hold, I know, but, hey, I can live with it.

A lot has changed since Boxing Day 2004. Life can turn out strange, eh? Nothing like you anticipated or planned or thought you deserved. But it is what you make of it that counts and, man, I'm still making it the best I can. If my story inspires just one person who has suffered depression, or had to overcome a drug or alcohol addiction, or felt unloved, unwanted, unworthy or incapable of shaking themselves out of the hole they seem to be in, I'd be so happy.

I know I am still far from perfect, and my family will attest to that. But what I have learned is that there is always someone out there worse off than you, always someone or something you can do to help. You don't need to wait for an invitation or instruction or to travel somewhere else in the world to find it. Sometimes it can be right in front of your eyes – like on the TV news tonight – if you can bring yourself to open them.

16

'IT COULD HAVE BEEN YOUR FUNERAL'

I thought I was having a heart attack. The pain in my chest was excruciating. In fact if I'd been a first-aid officer assessing someone with my symptoms, I would have said they were definitely suffering a heart attack. I had a 'heavy arm', like someone was sitting on it, and a sharp pain in the left side of my chest that tracked across to behind my sternum.

It was 21 February 2009 and happened while Tracey and I were at home watching television. Tracey was quite concerned and wanted to call an ambulance instantly; I was happy for her to drive me to hospital at first but the pain just got too much. The ambos came and put me straight on the ECG machine, gave me painkillers and when I got to John Hunter Hospital I was put straight through as a priority patient and put on a drip. Because of my past medical history they had trouble getting my pain under control and gave me a 10mg dose of Ketamine, which tripped me out; I was hallucinating. The medical team was fantastic. With my history they had to explore first whether it was a psychological thing, a conscious or unconscious avenue to get some drugs, and I accepted that. They soon realised the pain was real bloody real.

A CAT scan showed I'd suffered a pulmonary embolism. Part of a clot in my right calf had travelled up to my lungs. The doctor didn't muck around, he said bluntly, 'If the clot had gone to your heart or your head, you would have been going to a funeral not a hospital – your funeral.' It was that serious.

What had happened was that I had flown from Sydney to Lismore in the far north of New South Wales for a showing of *The Third Wave* and to talk about it afterwards. I should have known it was going to be an ill-fated trip because there was some problem with the film and they couldn't show the end of it. I'd had a really painful calf before that but I just thought it was soreness from the physiotherapy I was doing four days a week since the knee operation a couple of months earlier. I was getting pain in my shin too.

'IT COULD HAVE BEEN YOUR FUNERAL'

Anyway it seems like clots may have formed while I was idle for four or five days in intensive care when I had my knee replacement. The plane trip from Sydney to Lismore (just over an hour) and the train journeys from Newcastle to Sydney and return (two and a half hours each way) aggravated it and a piece broke off a clot and travelled up to my lung. It was a week after the return flight when I got rushed to hospital.

It was found I suffer from a fairly rare condition called primary antiphospholipid antibody syndrome, which is more prevalent in women than men. It's hard to explain but basically my body is far more prone to blood clots than is usual and reacts differently when they occur. It's genetic too, which is a problem for the kids; they will have to be tested regularly.

I had blood clots develop after the first lot of operations on my knee when I was in the army all those years ago, and on another occasion when I went to the dentist, and in hindsight I reckon that's what I had when my calf cramped up and gave me almighty pain the day I collapsed in Peraliya. So I had a history of a bit of danger and I was certainly conscious of it.

I was in hospital for ten days and even after I was allowed home I had to have Clexane injections into my stomach every day and take Warfarin tablets until my I and R level (the measure of coagulation in the blood) went up and stabilised in the safe zone, at a reading between 2 and 3. Mine was stuck at around 1.4 for two weeks after I was rushed to hospital. When I travel by plane I have to have a Clexane injection, take Warfarin and wear a stocking. It is a condition I have to be acutely aware of, but can live with it without too much difficulty.

The other pain I underwent before completing this book was a mental one. A lot of issues I thought I had put behind me came flooding back in the process of writing this book – it was pretty torturous. I thought I had dealt with them but I now realise there will never be a time when I won't have a flashback or a deeply disturbing memory about some of the experiences with death that I have had.

Sometimes when I have these flashbacks they are so real it is scary. I can feel it and smell them as though I am back there. When I hear a siren it can freak me out and I go back to seeing Simon or the other dead guy in Perth, or the tuk-tuk smashed up on the road near Galle. I have no control over it and that is the most frightening thing. It can come from nowhere; completely unexpectedly.

Other times a night-time dream will turn into a vivid nightmare and I will wake up covered in a lather of sweat, trembling and crying; I might scream out, 'Help me, help me.' Tracey can vouch for the fact that those nightmares became far more frequent while I had to delve into my past writing this book. Yet in some ways reliving these things has been therapeutic, too: I would never talk about them years ago and would keep them all inside but now if I'm talking about them that helps get them out of me. The more accepting I am that I did as much as I possibly could have and that I have to ignore the 'what ifs' that drove me crazy for so long, the closer to recovery I am. Seeing it on paper as this book took shape also added a bit of perspective that I didn't always have before.

It's twenty-two years now since I saw Simon die but the memories of it and his face are so vivid it's freaky. I actually booked in to see a psychiatrist after my scare with the blood clot.

A further trauma hit our lives in April 2009 when it was revealed Cory now suffers clinical depression. We received a phone call from Cory the morning Newcastle was due to play Manly at home and he put the club's doctor, Neil Halpin, on. Dr Halpin asked Tracey and me to come in for a chat about Cory. He informed us Cory was suffering clinical depression, that it was a genetic disease caused by a chemical imbalance, and that he needed medication and counselling to get through it.

It blindsided me; absolutely hit me for six. I didn't see it coming. I was more worried that perhaps one of the girls might have trouble with depression, if anyone. I had had a bit of a feeling all was not right when Cory told me once he had to take Valium to help him slow down after a game. That obviously worried me but then again a lot of high-intensity sportsmen have that trouble after an event, coming off the big adrenalin rush. Tracey had a stronger inkling that Cory wasn't himself; typical of mother's intuition and the fact they are so close.

His depression was partly caused by post-traumatic stress from what I put him through when he was child, so naturally I've beaten myself up over that. I might have given him some good stuff like his sporting genes, but the bad shit as well. I felt terrible guilt, remorse and shame; it hit me – all our family really – very hard for quite a few weeks. But Cory was so encouraging, telling me I had to get over it; that he has forgiven me and I need to forgive myself, and that means so much to me.

I can't deny that some of the contents of this, which Cory read before publication, plus him writing the foreword, brought a lot of bad memories back to the surface for him – was a catalyst for his depression to come out – and I feel rotten about that. I offered to stop the publication of this book if he felt it would relieve some of his pain. There is no way I would have continued with it if Cory didn't want me to. He feels my story has to be told warts and all because it is ultimately a positive one that other people who suffer depression might learn from. I respect that; he's a wonderful, brave young man who I am very proud of, as I am of Karah and Krystal.

Cory spent a week in Lake Macquarie Private Hospital getting treatment and counselling, and has been working through the disease since. It's nothing to be ashamed of; it's an illness that can hit anyone. He's back on the field now and, take it from me, he'll be the player he was before; even better. He's had great support from the club – from coach Brian Smith and football manager Warren Smiles – right through to the administration people and his team-mates.

NRL footballers go through a fair bit of pressure anyway, and Cory had the additional pressure of try-outs with the NFL in America, a few injuries that needed surgery, growing expectations about his career, and this book candidly revealing my life – it just all became too much for him. But one blessing is that he has confronted his illness and got the right advice at age twenty-one, whereas I was in denial and let it eat me up inside for far too long before doing something about it. Cory can avoid years of that sort of pain by being proactive. I'm at least thankful for that and wish I'd had the advice he has received when I was his age.

What I really want to get across is that there is no shame in having to seek help and there is certainly no use trying to deal with mental health problems all by yourself. Don't bury traumas inside you, whether it is a shocking car accident, the death of someone close to you, something like what the cricketers and umpires were confronted with by terrorists in Pakistan in 2009 or the people who were so tragically affected by the Victorian bushfires. Trauma is real, not perceived, and visiting specialists for counselling can be so worthwhile.

Whether you feel depressed yourself, or know someone who is suffering from depression or you suspect is affected by a serious mood disorder, don't be ashamed of it and stick your head in the sand. Having a 'macho' attitude and thinking you are soft if you can't handle things by yourself is just bullshit – and so self-defeating. There are organisations like Beyond Blue (beyondblue.org.au) and the Black Dog Institute (blackdoginstitute.org.au) which are easily contactable and do a fantastic amount of good work.

On top of my medical challenges, with a knee that is painful and now the blood clot problem, I continue to take tablets daily for depression. I'm not proud or glad about that but I'm not ashamed of it either. I know I am a better person when I stick with the medication – I am a better person for me and for those around me.

A WIFE'S OUTLOOK

By Tracey Paterson

It was quite surreal watching Donny Paterson, the character, in *The Third Wave*. I saw the man (although much older and balder!) that I married: the assertive, confident man; a natural leader who knew what he wanted and needed. I hadn't seen that Donny Paterson for a long while. He'd been taken away and Donny had given up searching for him. So I am so proud of what he did there, and so happy that the real Donny re-emerged – he found himself.

Countering all that, though, I have to admit I felt a little short-changed too. I was left thinking how it would be great to see that character surface a lot more often at home. Here was this hero-like character who was so responsible and receptive to all these others' daily needs – more than those he loves most who were sitting at home. I'd like a little more of that Donny daily, please. But, hey, I won't give up waiting; I think I've proved I'm not one to give up and I'm glad I haven't.

Don't get me wrong; Donny the person now is more focused, more driven and has a lot more motivation. I see the spark in his eyes again; I can see life behind those eyes now too. To see him have all this energy and self-esteem and passionate drive is wonderful, and we're all so proud to see that in his nature again because we are the only ones who know where he has come from and where he wants to go. But when you want to save the world, you have to start at home sometimes, that's all I'm saying.

Years ago I would say there were two Donnies; now there are three. I loved one man that I will never get back. He grew into another man, because of circumstance, that I am glad is now gone. Now he is another man altogether again, one who just wants to help others no matter where they are or how poor or unfortunate they are.

Donny was my first love and that's probably why I fell so deeply for him. I was very shy; I didn't strive for anything and just settled for enjoying life. And I wanted to marry a man who would take care of me. Donny was that man. He had a drive about him, a decisive nature without being dictatorial; he was so strong in himself and sure of himself.

I can track down so clearly now when he started to change – after Simon died in his arms and then he saw the other young man dead in his car. He just didn't seem to cope very well anymore; things just started to unravel slowly and I couldn't put my finger on it for a long while. He started to drink more heavily; he wanted to hang out with his mates and drink so he could forget, so he could numb himself. He then began to second guess himself a lot more. He retreated within himself.

The weaker he got, the stronger and more independent I got. There were many times when Donny became dependent on me, almost like a child. I became who am I now – colder in some ways, more questioning and less trusting – because of Don's illness. My spark, the excitement, was taken from me because I always needed to be the responsible one in the relationship. Due to circumstances I stopped becoming spontaneous and fun and just existed to look out for the kids and Donny; I was in constant survival mode. I became a detective and I challenged everything that came out of his mouth. I even went as far as pressing redial on the phone after he'd made a call to find out who he'd been talking to. In some ways I became very arrogant, and certainly more outspoken in regard to how Donny was treated medically; he wouldn't question things so I had to. Those things all happen when you live with someone who suffers an addiction. However, I came from a broken home with my parents' divorce and I was determined that I would never put my kids through that, so I kept surviving.

Beyond that, though, there was a good man inside and I yearned for him to come out of the shadow. He did in Peraliya. In Sri Lanka he had no one else to lean on, he had to take the initiative and stand up without the safety net he'd learned to rely on back home – and he certainly knew what he was doing because of his army training. You also see that confidence in his first-aid role; if I had a heart attack, Donny would be the person I'd want beside me. At home, though, maybe he just got used to me being the dominant one who organised everything and would challenge things. He is still too submissive at times and just lets things ride, lets me organise and doesn't question things. It's a real contradiction to what people see on the screen in *The Third Wave* or at the footy on a weekend.

He has suffered so badly from physical pain because of the injuries he sustained in the army, and the psychological pain of Simon's death and other traumas. During the times he was in hospital the morphine and pethidine took the pain away; he would at times exaggerate the extent of his pain when asked just so he could get more drugs into his system to take him 'away'. I suspected something was wrong; his mood swings were significant and he would leave home saying he was going to the gym or working late – I couldn't put my finger on what was going on, but I later learned he'd be out doing the rounds of the doctors' surgeries. When he left home he'd be strung out and on edge, but when he came back he was more together and relaxed.

It wasn't until the day after he broke into the doctor's surgery – and he was so ashamed of himself for that, and still is – that he told me he had a problem and what he had done. We sat down and talked and we both cried. I rang up the drug information line and was told he had to be reported and that it meant he would go on a national register. That never slowed up his ability to get the drugs because there wasn't a computer register at that time. All it did was formally brand him as a drug user.

The toughest part of those years, like it is for any woman with a husband who is an abuser of alcohol or substances, was the physical abuse. The emotional side of things got harder and harder, too, but I clung to the hope that somewhere inside there was still the man I married. When he finally went to the Perth clinic, I'd reached the end. I couldn't live that life anymore. I'd been struggling for four years with the decision whether to end our marriage or not but the 'what ifs' haunted me. Could I look my kids in the eyes and know I gave 110 per cent to keep the family together? I couldn't have lived with it if Don had committed suicide and I hadn't done enough to keep him alive as their father. In the end it was the obligation of keeping my kids safe and him alive that kept me in the relationship.

Before he went to Sri Lanka Donny existed – for Cory's football, for the girls and me. But he didn't live. He was always searching for something and felt he was missing something. As a family it wasn't perfect but we have always been very good at supporting each other. Few people knew about Don's condition, purely because I drummed into the kids that what happened in our house stayed there; I'd built a picket fence around our house to keep any troubles we had inside it. Still, he is very loving and supportive and often tells the kids how proud he is of them; he truly loves them, and me, and we know that. And we love him back just as much.

However, even when he came back after his first stint in Peraliya he was wrestling with himself – with the physical pain, because his body had taken a beating over there, plus his depression was bad because he had been off his medication. I'm sure he didn't intend to, but he nearly overdosed then. When he was suffering extreme pain, he would do anything to escape it; it became a one-track-mind issue, and the obvious way to nullify his pain was to pump painkillers into himself.

The thing with Donny is that he knows what he should and shouldn't do physically and how certain activities will affect him pain-wise. But because he wants to contribute to society and not sit on the lounge like others with similar disabilities, he will go and help out somewhere knowing it will come back to bite him. With football, for example, he would help out on Saturdays and Sundays knowing that Monday to Wednesday he would be in excruciating pain. For having two days of feeling 'relatively normal' (even though he runs like a duck onto the field), and 'contributing' and socialising, he knew the 'reward' was that he would be in agony for three days, having to lie on the couch with his legs elevated, and we would have a miserable person in our midst. He had such a strong relationship with Cory with their footy, a real male-bonding thing – you know, the boys together – but it got to the stage where it meant that come Tuesdays and Thursdays he couldn't even take Cory to training and wait for him. Physically and mentally he was spent and couldn't do it anymore, even though he wanted so badly to. That hurt both of them.

That was the case until October 2008 when he had the knee surgery. His time in Peraliya turned him around mentally, and that operation turned him around physically. As I write this he's had one weekend doing the first-aid at Newcastle Wests juniors and he didn't complain once about his pain afterwards, and was quite active in the ensuing days.

Donny is a new man, there's no doubt. He's a bit of a larger-than-life super-hero figure to some but he still avoids taking on responsibility at times, in everyday things. That doesn't come easily to him anymore. It does come easy when he's out in the field, so to speak, be it on the football field of a weekend or in Sri Lanka or Laos or on the streets of Newcastle at night helping street kids. At home – hmm! Maybe that's very much an Australian male thing, I don't know, but after the journey we've had – a hell of a journey, as you have just read – that's the only complaint I have now. I'm glad I have stuck by his side, for his sake, my sake and our three children's sake. And our journey has a long way to go yet, I hope – maybe he might take me with him for an overseas adventure, or even a holiday?

ACKNOWLEDGEMENTS

Mostly I'd like to thank my co-author, Neil Cadigan, for backing this book idea from the start, finding a publisher and believing in my story; I feel honoured that he has been my partner in this exercise.

I dearly thank Brigitta Doyle from ABC Books for her enthusiasm from the first time we approached her, and to all at ABC Books/HarperCollins for the great support they have given.

To Alison Thompson, Oscar Gubernati and Bruce French (and some other of the volunteers), thanks for helping me with information and photos from our wonderful experience together in Sri Lanka, especially Alison who is having her own book published in the USA – you are an inspiring lady. Thanks also go to Craig Pearce, who helped me bring this book to fruition, and my good mates John Killian and David Beljaars, who acted as sounding boards and have been terrific support for a long while.

The original idea of this book came from my wife, Tracey. She pushed me to pursue it, believing there was a good story there and that it should be told, even though it involved so much personal material about our family. And last but not least, my sincere appreciation to Karah, Krystal and Cory, who encouraged me during the process, even though it was tough and a bit painful at times.

ABOUT THE AUTHORS

Donny Paterson is a former Australian army engineer. Following the 2004 Boxing Day tsunami he travelled to Sri Lanka to volunteer for the rescue effort. He is currently involved with the relief agency he helped establish, Brick-Aid, and in NSW junior rugby league.

Neil Cadigan is a respected rugby league journalist and author. A former editor of *Big League* magazine, and NSW editor of *Rugby League Week*, he has also worked as CEO of English club Wakefield and as marketing manager of the Newcastle Knights and Hunter Mariners. A former Australian Sports Writer of the Year, Neil's previous books include autobiographies of Parramatta legends Ray Price and Brett Kenny, Newcastle Knights superstar Andrew Johns, and Olympic swimmer Brooke Hanson.